Cambridge Elements ≡

Elements in Religion and Violence
edited by
James R. Lewis
Wuhan University
Margo Kitts
Hawai'i Pacific University

EVOLUTIONARY PERSPECTIVES ON RELIGION AND VIOLENCE

Candace Alcorta
University of Connecticut

Richard Sosis
University of Connecticut

CAMBRIDGE
UNIVERSITY PRESS

CAMBRIDGE
UNIVERSITY PRESS

Shaftesbury Road, Cambridge CB2 8EA, United Kingdom

One Liberty Plaza, 20th Floor, New York, NY 10006, USA

477 Williamstown Road, Port Melbourne, VIC 3207, Australia

314–321, 3rd Floor, Plot 3, Splendor Forum, Jasola District Centre,
New Delhi – 110025, India

103 Penang Road, #05–06/07, Visioncrest Commercial, Singapore 238467

Cambridge University Press is part of Cambridge University Press & Assessment,
a department of the University of Cambridge.

We share the University's mission to contribute to society through the pursuit of
education, learning and research at the highest international levels of excellence.

www.cambridge.org
Information on this title: www.cambridge.org/9781009238342
DOI: 10.1017/9781009238328

First published 2022

A catalogue record for this publication is available from the British Library.

ISBN 978-1-009-23834-2 Paperback
ISSN 2397-9496 (online)
ISSN 2514-3786 (print)

Evolutionary Perspectives on Religion and Violence

Elements in Religion and Violence

DOI: 10.1017/9781009238328

First published online: August 2022

Candace Alcorta

University of Connecticut

Richard Sosis

University of Connecticut

Author for correspondence: Candace Alcorta, candace.alcorta@uconn.edu

ABSTRACT: Religion and violence share a complex and enduring history. Viewing violence and religion from an evolutionary perspective situates both within a broader framework of aggressive, affiliative, and signaling behaviors across species. In this work, the authors review genetic, epigenetic, and environmental factors that influence violence, distinguishing two types of aggression that differ in underlying physiology and intent. The use of communicative signals to delimit aggression across species is surveyed and the emergence of human symbolic ritual as a signaling system for creating alliances and promoting in-group cooperation is proposed. Using Wallace's typology of religion, this Element explores differences across religious systems in relation to socioecological variation and examines the underlying mechanisms by which religion "works." The use of violence as both an "honest signal" and a mechanism for inculcating religious belief is discussed, and the use of religion to incite, validate, and justify violence is reviewed.

KEYWORDS: religion, violence, human evolution, ritual, costly signaling

ISBNs: 9781009238342 (PB), 9781009238328 (OC)

ISSNs: 2397-9496 (online), 2514-3786 (print)

Contents

1 Introduction

On September 11, 2001, life in the United States was fundamentally transformed when nineteen young men hijacked four commercial aircrafts and perpetrated a multi-pronged attack on the World Trade Center in New York City and the Pentagon in Washington, DC. That attack killed nearly 3,000 unsuspecting men, women, and children in a single day and had profound impacts on both the United States and the world. The 9/11 bombings not only shattered America's perceived chimera of invincibility, they also nourished a wave of violent religious suicide terrorism across the world. Over the two decades prior to 9/11, a total of 188 suicide attacks occurred (Pape 2005); during the three years following 9/11, more than 300 such assaults killed more than 5,300 people in seventeen different countries. Unlike the earlier attacks, at least 70 percent of these more recent assaults were religiously motivated (Atran 2004:69).

Since 9/11 much scholarly research has focused on the role of religion in motivating terrorism. Predominant Western stereotypes of suicide terrorists as either desperate or deranged have been largely refuted by this research. Anthropologist and terrorism expert Scott Atran notes, "study after study demonstrates that suicide terrorists and their supporters are not abjectly poor, illiterate, or socially estranged" (Atran 2004:75). Nor do they exhibit a distinctive "suicide terrorist" psychological profile or personality (Hudson 1999). What is shared by most suicide terrorists, both secular and religious, are certain demographic characteristics – nearly all are young, male, and unattached. Religiously motivated terrorists share an additional experience, as well. Atran reports "more than 80 percent of known jihadis currently live in diaspora communities, which are often marginalized from the host society and physically disconnected from each other" (2006:135). In the governmental report, *The Sociology and Psychology of Terrorism: Who Becomes a Terrorist and Why?* author Rex Hudson concludes "Terrorists are generally people who feel alienated from society and have a grievance or regard themselves as victims of an injustice" (Hudson 1999:50).

Religiously motivated terrorism and the research it has engendered offer important insights into the paradoxical relationship between religion and violence. Yet, such terrorism is certainly not the only manifestation of religious violence. The ethnographic, archaeological, and historical records portray a long and complex relationship between religion and violence across diverse cultures and societies throughout human evolution. Violent shamanic rituals aimed at dispelling demons and appeasing spirits, harrowing tribal initiation ceremonies requiring tooth ablations, painful piercings, scarifications, and genital mutilations, and the martyrdom and religious wars of monotheistic World Religions together illustrate the ubiquity, tenacity, and diversity of the religion–violence relationship.

Numerous theories have been advanced to explain the complex and persistent relationship between religion and violence. Beginning with the classic work of Emile Durkheim, sociologists and religious study scholars, including terrorism experts Mark Juergensmeyer, Michael Jerryson, and Margo Kitts, have examined religious violence vis-a-vis the norms and needs of the social group. Social theorists, including Freud, Marx, and Baudrillard, viewed religious violence through the lens of power, emphasizing both its performative and political functions. Other scholars, such as Ariel Glucklich, Victor Turner, and Harvey Whitehouse, have focused on the psychological effects of religious violence on the individual. Anthropologists Andrew Strathern and Pamela Stewart (2005) discuss the role of "the imaginary" on violence and more specifically on what Juergensmeyer (2003) has termed "the mind of God" in relation to religious violence. And prominent historians, notably Walter Burkert and Rene Girard, have argued that religion is rooted in violence, with the ritual act of sacrifice comprising the very genesis of religious systems. More recently, evolutionary scientists, such as Joseph Bulbulia, John Shaver, and the authors of this volume, have utilized the framework of evolutionary theory to examine the religion–violence relationship.

The sections that follow summarize much of this work with particular focus on evolutionary scholarship. We begin by deconstructing violence and religion separately, aiming to assess their evolutionary development and adaptive functions. We then turn toward understanding variation in religions cross-culturally by examining the socioecological factors that can explain this variation. Next, we clarify how religions work; that is, we explore the underlying mechanisms that are essential for religions to operate. Understanding how religions work and how they evolved will provide us with a framework for understanding the complex relationship between religion and violence, which we address extensively in the penultimate section of this Element. We rely on diverse sets of data from ethnography, archaeology, primatology, psychology, neuroscience, and other fields, and in the final section we draw these data together and summarize how an evolutionary perspective helps explain the unfortunate, but real, relationship between religion and violence.

Throughout this work we employ a simple but important framework that was first introduced to evolutionary biology by the ethologist and Nobel laureate Niko Tinbergen. Tinbergen argued that when answering questions about the behavior of an organism it is vital to distinguish between what has become known as proximate-level and ultimate-level explanations. The former deals with the underlying causal mechanisms that produce behavior, including cognition, physiology, and neurology. Proximate-level explanations answer questions about *how* behaviors are produced. Ultimate-level explanations, on the other hand, answer questions about *why* a behavior evolved. They address questions about the phylogenetic history of a behavior – in other words, where a behavioral trait came from – as well as the survival and reproductive function of a behavior, that is, its adaptive value. Proximate and ultimate explanations are complementary and as will become quickly evident, we think both types of explanations are critical for understanding the religion–violence relationship.

Religion and violence have a complex and enduring history throughout human evolution. Unraveling the relationship between them requires that we first deconstruct the occurrence and function of each, both across species and throughout human evolution. This is where we begin.

2 What Is Violence?

Violence has long been a feature of human life. Phylogenetic studies demonstrate "a genetic component with high heritability" for human aggression (Gomez et al. 2016:233), a propensity shared with our closest primate kin, as well as with other social carnivores (Gomez et al. 2016: 233). And violence is manifest in many ways. Anthropologists, in their ethnographic fieldwork, have documented child and domestic abuse, rape, infanticide, revenge killings, intergroup raiding, and warfare across diverse cultures throughout the world.

What is violence? The Oxford English Dictionary (1989) defines violence as "The exercise of physical force so as to inflict injury on, or cause damage to, persons or property; action or conduct characterized by this; treatment or usage tending to cause bodily injury or forcibly interfering with personal freedom." In its *World Report on Violence and Health* (2002), the World Health Organization employs a somewhat different definition of violence: "The intentional use of physical force or power, threatened or actual, against oneself, another person, or against a group or community, that either results in or has a high likelihood of resulting in injury, death, psychological harm, maldevelopment, or deprivation" (World Health Organization 2002:4). The OED definition focuses on behavior. The WHO definition incorporates the additional requirement of "intent," an addition considered by some to be a critical feature separating human and nonhuman violence (Bushman 2018:iv–v).

It is, of course, currently impossible to ascertain the intent of nonhuman species engaging in aggression and violence. Nonverbal signals of aggression that convey such intent to conspecifics, however, are readily communicated across widely diverse species, including our own. Direct eye contact, bared teeth, and inflated body stance all communicate aggression in beagles, baboons, and bar brawlers alike. These aggressive behaviors are spontaneously and subconsciously motivated in response to threat and convey a clear message to potential aggressors. Neuroimaging data indicate that such signals are spontaneously and subconsciously processed by humans, as well.

Defining Violence from an Evolutionary Perspective

From an evolutionary perspective, it is not what individuals intend to do but what they, in fact, do that matters. Evolutionary scientists, therefore, typically employ definitions of violence that focus on observable behaviors rather than intent. Such definitions are able to encompass nonhuman species and they situate violence within an evolutionary framework, facilitating the examination of its impacts on individual fitness. Behaviorally based definitions offer additional advantages, as well. Observable behaviors can be empirically measured and recorded, providing the data necessary to compare aggressive and violent behaviors across individuals and species. Such data allow researchers to assess the influence of genetic, epigenetic, and environmental factors on violent behavior. This is vital for deconstructing and differentiating types of aggression and violence, as well as for identifying their proximate and ultimate causes.

Violence and aggression against conspecifics are certainly not unique to *Homo sapiens*. Numerous animals exhibit highly antagonistic behaviors, and many species engage in lethal violence, as well. Sharks cannibalize littermates in utero, axolotl amphibians eat the limbs of siblings, Nazca booby nestlings forcefully expel co-hatchlings and are, in turn, violently and sometimes lethally abused by adult males. We see similar patterns of violence among mammalian species. Wolves, for example, attack and kill other wolves in both intra and intergroup conflicts, and male lions taking over a new pride routinely commit infanticide. The primate order of which we are a part is rife with violence, from aggressive baboons to infanticidal langurs to lethally raiding chimpanzees. A survey conducted by biologist Jose Gomez and his colleagues found reports of lethal violence in 40 percent of mammalian species included in their sample of 5,020 extant and 5,747 extant and nearly extinct mammals (2016:233). While lethal violence was uncommon in some clades, including bats, whales, and lagomorphs, it was relatively frequent in others. Indeed, "even seemingly peaceful mammals such as hamsters and horses sometimes kill individuals of their own species" (2016, 233).

Violence in Human Evolution

Violence has been a frequent and ubiquitous occurrence across human societies, as well. Hannah Arendt notes "No one engaged in thought about history and politics can remain unaware of the enormous role violence has always played in human affairs" (1970:6). Archaeological evidence suggests that violence was likely present in human societies early in the emergence of our species. Evidence of blunt instrument trauma among our Neanderthal cousins indicates that our common ancestor likely engaged in violence. At the Spanish site of Sima de los Huesos dated around

250,000 years ago several skulls show evidence of impact fractures, with one cranium exhibiting thirteen healed fractures (Zollikofer et al. 2002:6444). While some have interpreted these findings as evidence of accidental trauma, recent taphonomic-forensic analysis concluded that the type and location of the fractures indicate intentional lesions rather than accidental trauma (Sala et al. 2022). Currently, the oldest fossil evidence of possible violence in early modern humans consists of a fossilized skull from the South African site of Klasies River dated at approximately 90,000 years ago. This skull exhibits a healed fracture suggestive of blunt instrument trauma, as well (Thorpe 2003:151). The depiction of anthropomorphic figures pierced by projectiles in Upper Paleolithic European cave art, as well as 13,000-year-old fossilized skeletons from Italy and Egypt bearing embedded flint points and quartzite bladelets also suggest human violence (Thorpe 2003: 152). At the 12,000-year-old site of Jebel Sahaba in the Sudan chert projectile points are prolific, with several of the twenty-four individuals exhibiting trauma characteristics. One woman in this assemblage shows evidence of at least a dozen wounds (Thorpe 2003: 152). At the slightly later Kenyan site of Nataruk dated around 10,000 years ago women and children were again the victims of brutal violence in a single attack. Eight females, five children, and a teenager are among the twenty-seven victims, including one pregnant woman bearing a young fetus. These slain hunter-gatherers suffered a particularly horrific end, with bound and broken knees and hands, bashed-in skulls and spear-pierced bodies (Lahr et al. 2016:395–396).

More recently, ethnographers have documented a long history of warfare among small-scale societies (Keeley 1996). Numerous hunter-gatherer and horticultural societies, such as the Arunta of Australia, the Yanomamo of South America, and the Ilahita Arapesh of New Guinea traditionally engaged in significant intra and intergroup violence. Violence was rife in early agricultural societies, as well. The extent of such violence is well illustrated by the Yamnaya invasion of Europe. These horsemen swept through agricultural Europe from the Eurasian steppes some 5,000 years ago. Genetic evidence shows that the Yamnaya warriors completely obliterated previous male lineages in some areas and "contributed to at least half of Europeans' genetic ancestry" (Gibbons 2017). Subsequent empires, from

Assyria to Rome to China to Peru, were bathed in the blood of soldiers, slaves, and sacrificial victims, while feudal societies from Germany to Japan were dominated by violent warlords.

Modern era warfare has continued to expand the scope and lethality of human violence through technological innovations and military might. Child and domestic abuse, homicides, and warfare continue to plague human societies across the globe. At the beginning of the twenty-first century violence was among the leading causes of death in the age group fifteen to forty-four years worldwide (World Health Organization 2002). Since 2001, warfare in major war zones throughout the Middle East alone has directly claimed the lives of some 800,000 individuals (Crawford and Lutz 2019). According to the World Health Organization's 2002 *Report on Violence and Health*, "Each year, more than 1.6 million people worldwide lose their lives to violence" (2002).

Violence and Aggression

Some researchers have characterized violence as pathological behavior. Several human disorders do demonstrate that violence may arise from pathology, yet the frequency and ubiquity of violence across numerous species suggest that not all violence is the product of pathology. Biologists, however, often consider violence to be an "extreme form of aggression" (Bushman 2018:v) and note that under some circumstances, "violence can be seen as an adaptive strategy, favouring the perpetrator's reproductive success in terms of mates, status or resources" (Gomez et al. 2016:233).

As primatologist Michael Wilson notes

> "Early observers of primate aggression, especially infanti-cide, cannibalism, and intergroup killing, regarded these behaviors as pathological or dysfunctional behaviors ... (yet) ... current evidence indicates that in most cases aggression follows evolutionary logic. Animals attack other animals when the costs of attacking are low or when the benefits are likely to be high ... aggression occurs when it is likely to benefit the reproductive success of the aggres-sor and/or the aggressor's kin" (Wilson 2003:182–183).

Infanticide in chimpanzees, langurs, and lions, as well as the intergroup raids observed in both wolves and chimpanzees illustrate such adaptive violence. In each of these cases the perpetrators of violence gain a fitness advantage. By killing the progeny of the defeated dominant male, lions and langurs simultaneously eliminate the genes of competitors and obtain increased mating opportunities by bringing previously nursing females into estrus sooner. Intergroup raids eliminate and/or weaken competitors, potentially expanding access to both resources and mates. Certainly, the surviving shark embryo, the cannibal axlotl, and the successful booby hatchling described earlier each have a monopoly on nutrients, thereby improving their respective somatic fitness. Violence, in general, and lethal violence in particular can enhance an individual's fitness through increased somatic benefits as well as expanded reproductive opportunities. Somatic and reproductive gains realized through violent behaviors may increase the fitness of close kin, as well, thereby enhancing one's own inclusive fitness.

Viewing violence as an extreme form of aggression situates it on a spectrum of increasingly agonistic behaviors. Aggression has been described as "the behavioral weapon of choice for individuals to gain and maintain access to desired resources (food, territory, mating partners), defend themselves and their progeny from rivals and predators, and establish and secure social status/hierarchical relationships" (de Boer 2018:81). This is applicable across numerous species and is true of human aggression, as well.

Two Types of Violence

Not all aggression is alike, a fact recognized by justice systems throughout the world. Cognitive psychologist Steven Pinker notes "biologists have long noted that the mammalian brain has distinct circuits that underlie very different kinds of aggression" (2011:497). Central among these different kinds of aggression are two very distinct types that differ "in their psychological, physiological, and biological manifestations as well as in etiology" (Zhu et al. 2019:7731). The defensive aggression of a lioness protecting her cubs is intuitively different from the infanticidal violence of the male seeking to kill them, although both reflect behaviors aimed at maximizing reproductive fitness. Biological anthropologist Richard Wrangham notes that these two distinctive "modes" of aggression activate "two different pathways in a key neural circuit underlying aggression" (Wrangham 2018:247). This circuit links limbic structures that function in threat appraisal and emotional processing with cortical areas of the brain responsible for such executive functions as social judgment, inhibition, and planning. While both types of aggression engage this corticolimbic circuit, each differentially activates specific structures within it.

The first "mode" of aggression, illustrated by the lioness defending her cubs, has been termed "reactive" or "defensive" aggression. Reactive aggression is a spontaneous emotional response to a perceived threat or thwarted objective (Zhu et al. 2019:7731). It enlists the body's "fight or flight" response and is marked by high arousal of the sympathetic nervous system. Reactive aggression is generally deemed to be defensive, impulsive, emotional, and affective. The goal of reactive aggression is to eliminate the provocation or threatening stimulus while incurring the least possible harm. It is characterized by species-typical behaviors with strong inhibitory feedback mechanisms, including "taboos, ritualization, submission, reconciliation and appeasement" (de Boer 2018:81). These behaviors "serve to keep physical aggression in control and prevent potentially adverse (i.e., injury or death) consequences" (de Boer 2018:81).

The second mode of aggression has been termed "proactive" or "offensive aggression." Unlike reactive aggression, proactive aggression does not occur in immediate reaction to a perceived threat, nor does it derive from activation of the "fight or flight" response. It is planned, purposeful, and goal oriented with the aim of achieving specific objectives for personal internal or external rewards. While reactive aggression is "always associated with anger, as well as with a sudden increase in sympathetic activation, a failure of cortical regulation, and an easy switching among targets" (Wrangham 2018:246), proactive aggression most frequently involves a low level of emotional and sympathetic arousal, is highly focused, with "attention to a consistent target" (Wrangham 2018:246), and is goal directed. In contrast to the "heat" and "passion" of reactive aggression, proactive aggression has been described as "cold" and "dispassionate." The usurping male lion that targets and kills unrelated newborns of the pride he has acquired, chimpanzees that purposefully stalk, kill, and dismember lone conspecifics from neighboring troops, and the human serial killer who carefully selects each victim and painstakingly plans each murder all engage in proactive aggression. Proactive aggression involves lower physiological arousal on the part of the aggressor, yet is likely to result in more lethal outcomes. Lack of social communication, the targeting of vulnerable body parts, and the goal-directed psychology of this type of aggression render it more akin to predation than to reactive aggression. Indeed, the same neural circuits that are activated during predatory behavior are engaged during proactive aggression (Wrangham 2018:247).

Genetics, Epigenetics, Stress, and the Environment

Laboratory research and human twin studies have shown that genetic and developmental factors significantly impact the propensity to engage in aggression, as well as the type of aggression displayed (Wrangham 2018:247). Some genotypes predispose individuals to reactive aggression when faced with adverse experiences (Lansford 2018:19). A key structure in the brain's "aggression circuit" is the orbitofrontal cortex (OFC) which is "crucially involved in responding to expectancies of social anger, (and) . . . knowledge of the other individual's position in the dominance hierarchy" (Blair and Charney 2003:26). Impaired OFC functioning, whether resulting from genetic, epigenetic, or physical injury, is associated with an increased propensity for reactive aggression (Blair and Charney 2003:23). Impacts of injury to the OFC are famously illustrated by the case of Phineas Gage, a railroad worker whose brain was damaged when a metal railroad rod shot through his skull. Following this event, the previously stolid, responsible, and conscientious railroad supervisor experienced both a loss of social inhibition and an increase in the propensity for reactive violence (Damasio 1994).

Genes that impact the brain's neurotransmitter systems alter the propensity for reactive aggression, as well. Serotonin is a key neurotransmitter in the corticolimbic brain circuit central to aggressive behavior. The serotonin system is complex with fourteen different receptor types differentially distributed across numerous brain structures. These subtypes perform different functions throughout the brain, with varying impacts on aggressive behavior. A complete understanding of the serotonin system has yet to be developed; however, a large body of research demonstrates that abnormalities in serotonin (5-HT) function specific to the corticolimbic circuit underlying aggression may "modify an individual's lability to impulsive aggression" (Lesch 2003:54). A recent review of serotonin studies conducted by Cocarro and colleagues led these researchers to conclude that "an extensive literature supports a role for serotonin in impulsive aggression (and suicidality). Evidence suggests that serotonin modulates activity in areas of the prefrontal cortex, including the orbitofrontal cortex and anterior cingulate, which are implicated in 'top-down' control of limbic responding to stimuli" (Cocarro et al. 2015:300). Low levels of serotonin in these areas have been associated with explosive aggression and impulsive violence in boys exhibiting conduct disorder (Lesch 2003:36).

Environmental factors impact a propensity for aggression, as well. Such factors have particularly pronounced effects during early development and adolescence. The neurological and endocrinological changes that occur during these developmentally sensitive periods are critical to attachment, stress, and emotional processing. Environmental factors that impact brain development during these "experience expectant" developmental periods may have profound effects on subsequent social and aggressive behaviors (Greenough 1986).

Stress and Aggression

One of the major environmental factors found to impact the propensity for aggressive behavior is stress. Stressful events, including ambiguity, frustration, threat, and danger, all initiate a powerful cascade of neurophysiological responses that impact brain function. Chronic stressors that increase plasma levels of glucocorticoids are associated with various physiological and psychological disorders, including severe depression and suicide (Marques et al. 2009). When chronic stress is experienced during sensitive developmental periods, such as childhood, it may ultimately result in lowered basal plasma glucocorticoid levels, a condition which has been implicated in subsequent aggressive behavior (Haller and Kruk 2003:105). Children repeatedly exposed to traumatic and frustrating experiences, particularly neglect, physical, and sexual abuse "react more quickly with anger to minor incidents and ... exhibit a higher level of aggression" (Barnow and Freyberger 2003:218). A clinical study of 100 depressed and/or anxious children found significantly lower levels of basal plasma cortisol in children traumatized by physical and/or sexual abuse as compared to non-traumatized children (Kellner et al. 2018:744). Likewise, research conducted by Haller and Kruk shows an inverse correlation between basal plasma cortisol levels and aggressiveness in children with conduct disorder (2003:105). Such glucocorticoid hypofunction-associated aggression is associated with high levels of anxiety, as well. Patients with post-traumatic stress disorder show both low basal levels of cortisol and heightened aggression (Haller and Kruk 2003:100–101).

These findings highlight a central role of glucocorticoid function in preparing to meet both short and long-term threats. While short-term increases in glucocorticoid function prime the body and provide the resources necessary to sustain the "fight or flight" response, long-term low levels of basal plasma cortisol resulting from ongoing stress are associated with both chronic anxiety and increased aggression. While stress responses have short-term adaptive value in preparing the body to assess and appropriately react to threat or danger, when these responses are repeated and sustained during sensitive developmental periods, they may "reset" endocrinological systems.

Laboratory studies of nonhuman species clearly demonstrate that "early life stress ... enhances adult anxiety-like behaviors and has a major impact on social and aggressive behaviors" (de Boer 2018:84). Early life social neglect in rodents results in numerous neurophysiological changes, including reduced gray matter density, functional alterations in the prefrontal cortex, exacerbated autonomic arousal, and a myriad of glucocorticoid stress responses. These changes manifest behaviorally in "abnormal and high levels of aggression, attacks on vulnerable body parts, (and) sudden unsignaled attacks" (de Boer 2018: 84). Animal and clinical studies demonstrate that sustained high cortisol levels alter serotonin uptake in the brain (Tafet et al. 2001). In nonhuman primates, low central nervous system serotonin activity has been associated with "impaired impulse control, unrestrained aggression, social isolation, and low social dominance" (Higley and Linnoila 1997: 39).

For humans, childhood maltreatment, including physical, sexual, and emotional abuse, as well as physical and emotional neglect, impacts numerous brain structures, as well. These may include decreases in hippocampal and prefrontal cortex volumes, reductions in fiber tracts including the corpus callosum, and alterations in sensory systems (Teicher et al. 2016:652). The hippocampus is responsible for memory processing. Cell death resulting from a sustained stress response reduces hippocampal volume, resulting in impaired memory and learning abilities (Teicher et al. 2003). Chronic stress also suppresses the brain's reward system and initiates an up-regulation of the amygdala, the brain nuclei responsible for threat and fear assessment and the initiation of aggression (Kaufman and Charney 2001; Sapolsky 1996). These brain changes behaviorally manifest in increased vigilance, inhibition of behavioral responses in novel settings, reduced affiliative behaviors, increased aggression, impaired cognition, and an increased susceptibility to drug and alcohol abuse (Teicher et al. 2016).

Maltreated children are likely to exhibit subsequent behavioral problems in adolescence and adulthood with childhood maltreatment constituting a major risk factor for adult psychopathology. Even in the absence of direct trauma and physical aggression, mere exposure to aggression and violence during childhood has been shown to impact subsequent aggressive behaviors. Children who have witnessed maternal abuse report aggressive incidents similar to those of abused children (Barnow and Freyberger 2003:219).

The epigenetic, neural, and endocrinological alterations that occur in response to childhood/adolescent abuse and trauma have serious social, psychological, and physical consequences. They are, however, likely to have evolved as adaptive mechanisms. Children continuously exposed to ongoing neglect and trauma need to be hypervigilant and aggressive to survive, as do individuals repeatedly exposed to traumatic events such as war. Faster brain maturation of children exposed to chronic stress has been suggested to be an adaptive response, as well (Tooley et al. 2021:372). For these individuals, the short-term benefits of increased vigilance, reduced thresholds for aggression in threatening and unstable environments, and the need to "grow up fast" outweigh the high long-term somatic and social costs incurred (Georgiev et al. 2013:678; Tooley et al. 2021:372).

Adolescence, Stress, and Aggression

Neurophysiological changes that occur during adolescence make this a vulnerable period for stress, as well. Extensive changes in both neurological and endocrinological systems occur during adolescence, creating a malleable substrate for environmental factors to impact the developing brain (Dahl 2004; Spear 2000). During adolescence ongoing maturation of the temporal and frontal cortices exert increasing control over the limbic circuits involved in aggressive, emotional, and social behaviors. The heightened emotionality of early adolescence is followed by ongoing changes in neurotransmitter systems that link cortical, limbic, and reward processing regions of the brain with serotonergic and dopaminergic reward systems assuming critical roles in this linkage. Ongoing maturation of temporal regions of the brain involved in social functions, and prefrontal regions responsible for executive functioning, occurs during later adolescence/ early adulthood. Maturation of these regions increasingly exerts "top down" control over limbic and reward systems, providing greater cortical control of impulse regulation, inhibition, social behavior and symbolic behavior, and planning. These neurophysiological changes, in tandem with myriad changes in hormonal systems, render adolescence a particularly vulnerable developmental period.

Adolescents are at high risk for a large range of social and psychological disorders, including alcohol and substance abuse, mental illness, gang violence, conduct disorder, internet addiction, juvenile delinquency, and suicide. Exposure to violence, abuse, and trauma experienced during adolescence may have long-lasting impacts (Alcorta 2021). A longitudinal study of 913 Finnish adolescents analyzed effects of trauma experienced from ages twelve to fourteen on violence at ages fifteen to seventeen. The study showed that "severe stress related to traumatic or strong negative life changes in adolescence is a risk factor for violent behaviour" (Peltonen 2020:845).

Violence experienced during adolescence may not have to be direct to exert long-lasting impacts on aggressive behavior. Lansford notes that "(a)n extensive body of research has demonstrated that viewing violent television programs and playing violent video games are predictive of an increase in physically aggressive behavior over time" (2018:18). Social learning and social information processes, including appraisal bias and moral disengagement have been implicated in these associations, particularly in relation to television and movie violence (Gini et al. 2014:56–68). Positive associations have been reported between prolonged time spent by adolescents on violent video gaming and aggression, as well (Villani and Joshi 2003:238–239). Small sample neuroimaging studies have found lower right orbitofrontal gray matter volume in excessive internet gamers (Zhou 2019:100), as well as changes in both gray and white matter of young male players of violent video games that "correlated with measures of aggression, hostility, self-esteem, and the degree of internet addiction" (Mohammadi et al. 2020).

Purported associations between violent video games and aggression are controversial, however. Studies showing correlations between video gaming and aggression have been challenged on methodological grounds (Adachi and Willoughby 2011) and a meta-analysis of research conducted by Ferguson and colleagues found only "negligible relationships between violent games and aggressive or prosocial behavior, (and) small relationships with aggressive affect and cognitions" (2020:1423). Yet, a 2020 research review conducted by the American Psychological Association (2020) led that body to conclude that "there is convergence of research findings across multiple methods and multiple samples with multiple types of measurements demonstrating the association between violent videogame use and both increases in aggressive behavior, aggressive affect, aggressive cognitions, and decreases in prosocial behavior, empathy, and moral engagement." Taken together this research suggests that, while violent video gaming by adolescents may be associated with increased aggression, additional research is required to identify both the nature and extent of such associations.

3 Social Groups, Signals, and Symbols

Violence may sometimes be an adaptive strategy; yet, the costs of aggression and violence can be considerable. Aggressive encounters require time and energy, and high-stakes endeavors may readily escalate to increased violence. Attackers who misjudge their opponents may lose status, be ostracized, sustain injuries, or even be killed. Few adversaries willingly go to their deaths.

Ongoing aggression not only impacts individuals, it also destabilizes social groups and disrupts functional social relationships. The uncertainty, ambiguity, and stress resulting from ongoing aggression and violence may impact the biological fitness of all group members. In-group aggression and violence render groups more vulnerable to outside attacks, with attendant risks for loss of mates, territory, and life. While aggression may sometimes be adaptive, it is not "invariant or even adaptive in all situations . . . the conditions under which violence benefits evolutionary fitness depend on the ecological and cultural context" (Gomez et al. 2016:233). Since the price of aggression can be high, individual fitness depends on the ability to accurately calculate potential costs. This requires a reliable assessment of the condition, motivation, and intent of potential adversaries.

Signals, Rituals, and Aggression

Throughout the animal kingdom species-specific signals have evolved for this purpose. These signals communicate important information regarding the condition, motivation, and intent of conspecifics. Indexical signals – signals that directly indicate what they represent – that derive from biological traits, such as the croak pitch of frogs and the musth signature of bull elephants, provide potential competitors with important information regarding the condition, motivation, and/or intent of adversaries. For frogs, the deeper the croak, the bigger the frog. For elephants, the stronger the musth, the greater the motivation to compete for mating rights. Behavioral signals, such as the eyelid flash and canine baring of male hamadryas baboons have also evolved to convey important information regarding condition, motivation, and aggressive intent. In response, gestures of submission serve to avoid or diminish aggressive encounters. Such signals decrease the costs of continuously reestablishing social and physical boundaries within social groups, thereby freeing time and resources for feeding, mating, and caretaking of young. They also delimit the costs of reactive aggression between adversaries, allowing winners to claim their spoils and losers to live and fight another day. When environmental conditions are relatively stable and signals cannot easily be "faked," such signals provide effective communication. However, when competition is increased due to ambiguous or degraded conditions, or when signals can be readily "faked," more elaborate signals are required to ensure signal "honesty" and improve signal reliability (Krebs and Dawkins 1984:380–402).

The costliest of animal signals in terms of time, energy, and somatic resources are ritualized displays (Krebs and Dawkins 1984: 380–402). Zahavi (1975:205) has argued that such costly signals provide honest information for receiver assessment since only those fit enough can bear their costs. From crayfish to corvids to macaques ritualized displays of aggression have evolved to communicate reliable information for combatants regarding the condition, motivation, and intent of their competitors. These displays entail time, energy, and resources and increase exposure to predation. Yet, such costly displays also optimize decision-making and provide a mechanism for deception detection, as well as delimiting and de-escalating aggression and violence.

Laboratory experiments indicate that the costliness of signaling is driven by receiver selection for reliable signals (Rowe 1999:921). Improving the reliability of communications requires: (1) focused receiver attention, (2) use of a common "language," (3) message patterning and order, (4) repetition, (5) redundancy, (6) multi-modality, and (7) relevance. Ritualized displays incorporate all these elements. They are costly in terms of time, energy, and increased vulnerability as a signaler. Yet, the formality, sequence, repetition, and patterning that increase the costs of ritual also improve the ability of the receiver to assess the reliability of the message transmitted. Ritual participation focuses attention, enhances memory, and promotes associational learning (Rowe 1999:927). As a result, the receiver is neurophysiologically "primed" for accurate assessment and appropriate action (Alcorta and Sosis 2005:31).

These same elements of ritual afford "deception detection," as well. An imposter may deceive the unwary or unconcerned, but deception of alerted and involved participants is a much more difficult undertaking. Concomitantly, while it is relatively easy to "lie" in a single mode of communication, maintenance of that "lie" becomes increasingly difficult when repetition and redundancy across modalities occur. Sequencing and patterning add further complexity to the communication, making deception even more difficult and costly to maintain (Alcorta and Sosis 2005:330). The embedding of costly signals in ritualized displays provides an additional means for assessment. Across many species, ritualized displays that incorporate such "hard to fake" signals afford an additional component of communication. For example, the exuberant tails of peacocks so brilliantly displayed in courtship rituals reliably communicate male fitness since color intensity is inversely correlated with parasite load and plumage condition is a function of fitness. Likewise, the direct stare, piloerection, and chest beating of gorillas convey important information regarding motivation and intent, but they also afford potential combatants an opportunity to clearly assess the physical condition of their opponent. Humans, too, employ costly ritualized displays that incorporate signals that reliably convey the signaler's condition, motivation, and intent. Knit eyebrows over a glaring stare, bared teeth and an open mouth, and a menacing stance with a raised fist all signal aggression in bar rooms and boardrooms alike.

The structure of ritual neurophysiologically primes participants to accurately receive and assess information, while the embedded signals of ritual elicit behavioral responses. Some signals elicit innate species-specific fixed action pattern responses, such as the "head-pumping" and "rolling" of Canadian geese. Other signals are ontogenetic, requiring the development of an innate predisposition through social learning. The courtship songs of passerines and culturally distinctive group songs of humpback whales are examples of such learned signals. Ritualized displays incorporating such signals serve numerous functions but are particularly important in relation to courtship and reactive aggression. In the latter case, the ritualized use of species-specific signals to communicate intent and terminate aggression can mean the difference between life and death.

Ritual and Violence in Our Primate Kin

The role of ritual in delimiting and de-escalating aggression is well illustrated by our two closest living primate relatives, the chimpanzee

(*Pan troglodytes*) and the bonobo (*Pan paniscus*). The human lineage diverged from the common ancestor of chimps and bonobos some 5–7 million years ago. Chimpanzee and bonobo lineages diverged from one another around 2 million years ago and share approximately 99.6 percent of their DNA (Prufer et al. 2012:527). These two primates are so physically similar that they were considered the same species until quite recently.

While chimpanzees and bonobos share nearly all their DNA, the ecologies of the two species differ, as does their social organization. Bonobos inhabit a relatively small, delimited territory in the humid tropical forests south of the Congo River in the Democratic Republic of Congo. They are largely frugivorous but consume a wide variety of other foods, including small vertebrates. Chimpanzees inhabit a much larger habitat of more open, dry grasslands across a large swath of equatorial Africa. They are omnivorous, consuming a wide variety of plant and animal species. Divergence in the ancestral species leading to chimps and bonobos likely occurred due to geographic separation when the Congo River formed, splitting the ancestral population into two groups (Prufer et al. 2012:528).

Chimpanzees and bonobos both live in social groups of approximately thirty individuals, on average, although troops of up to ninety individuals have been observed. Chimpanzee troops are dominated by kin-related males who remain in their natal troop and aggressively maintain male-centered dominance hierarchies, as well as strong intermale alliances. Bonobo males also remain in their natal group throughout life. In contrast to chimpanzee troops, however, it is affiliative female associations that form the core of bonobo groups with males "commonly subordinate to females" (Prufer et al. 2012:527). Bonobo males retain closer ties to their mothers than to other males within the troop, and it is the mother's position within the social hierarchy that determines their rank. Hugging and kissing are engaged in by both bonobos and chimpanzees for post-conflict reconciliation. For bonobos, however, genital stimulation and other sexualized behaviors play a large role in everyday social relationships. Bonobo matriarchal female associations are largely created and sustained through affiliative, sexualized behaviors. These behaviors diffuse potentially aggressive situations and create and maintain female alliances.

Both chimpanzees and bonobos engage in bouts of reactive aggression as dyads fight over mates, food, or dominance. Although the frequency of such bouts is somewhat similar in the two species, the severity of reactive aggression is much greater in chimpanzees than bonobos. Wild male bonobos are less aggressive than wild chimpanzee males, while female bonobos are aggressive at higher rates than their chimpanzee counterparts (Wrangham 2018:248). Violence between the sexes differs between the two species, as well. In chimpanzee society, "every adult female is regularly attacked by every young male as he moves into the adult hierarchy," with continuing attacks throughout life. In contrast, bonobo females "win more conflicts than males, who are mostly subordinate to females and do not regularly attack them" (Wrangham 2018:248).

As in all other great apes, female chimps and bonobos leave the troop at adolescence to join new troops. Chimpanzee females entering a new troop must integrate into a male-dominated society in which unrelated females actively compete for resources for both themselves and their offspring. Primatologists Ann Pusey and Kara Schroepfer-Walker report, "Females are aggressive to immigrant females and even kill the newborn infants of community members. The intensity of such aggression correlates with population density" (Pusey and Schroepfer-Walker 2013). The situation for female adolescents migrating to new bonobo groups is quite different. For these adolescents, group membership is dependent upon creating bonds with the dominant females of the group. This is achieved through affiliative, sexualized submission behaviors.

The marked differences in social organization between chimpanzees and bonobos are also reflected in the levels of proactive aggression exhibited by the two species (Wrangham 2018:248). In contrast to the infanticide and often lethal male intergroup raids that typify chimpanzee society, infanticide among bonobos is nonexistent, intergroup aggression is rare, there is no evidence of lethal aggression toward conspecifics and "no proactive aggression leading to intergroup killings has been observed, despite ample opportunity to make relevant observations" (Wrangham 2018: 248). Rather, aggressive encounters both within and between bonobo troops are de-escalated through the performance of highly sexualized affiliative rituals.

Like both chimpanzees and bonobos, humans exhibit "a significant phylogenetic signal for lethal violence" (Gomez et al. 2016:233). Pinker has noted that the intergroup raids of many hunter-gatherer and horticultural societies bear "an uncanny resemblance" to the intergroup raids of chimpanzees (2011:488). At the same time, the frequency of in-group fighting in human small-scale societies is much lower than that observed in either chimp or bonobo societies (Wrangham 2018:248). Wrangham has argued that human evolution has been marked by decreasing rates of reactive aggression and increasing rates of proactive aggression (Wrangham 2019:9). A broad survey of human violence across cultures and throughout history has led Pinker to conclude that human violence has declined as increasingly large, complex, and interdependent societies create, impose, and enforce social structure and order (2011:xxiv–xxv). These two models are not incompatible. Ongoing reduction of reactive intragroup aggression in human groups may well be accompanied by increasing intergroup proactive aggression. As social groups grow larger, it would, therefore, be expected that human violence would decline. This does, however, depend on the ability to create and sustain large cooperative nonkin groups over both space and time. Contemporary nation-states achieve this through powerful political systems capable of controlling in-group aggression and monopolizing proactive, out-group aggression. Yet, both modern history and current global politics demonstrate that new nation-states struggle to achieve such power, and even well-established polities face ongoing problems of internal dissension, fragmentation, and insurrection. If these problems confront well-financed and highly militarized modern nation-states, how did earlier human societies overcome the inherent challenges of in-group aggression and cooperation? For many evolutionary anthropologists, religion provides the answers to these questions.

4 What Is Religion?

Religion is a universal feature of human societies. Yet, like violence, religion is notoriously difficult to define. From an evolutionary perspective, it is equally difficult to explain. The supernatural agents and counterintuitive beliefs of religion are deemed irrational by many, abstruse by most, and impervious to empirical validation by all. Moreover, religious rites and sacred obligations demand investments of time, energy, and resources that could profitably be expended on pragmatic secular enterprises. Religious practices frequently inflict pain and suffering on adherents and require numerous sacrifices. Researchers have long wondered how a cultural institution with unverifiable beliefs and such demanding expenditures could have survived throughout human history. What is religion and why is it a recurrent element of human societies everywhere?

Over the past several centuries numerous definitions of religion have been proposed, yet a widely accepted consensus remains elusive. Not only do different researchers bring diverse interests and perspectives to the study of religion; religions themselves differ greatly from one another, both across cultures and across time. The shamanic religions of hunter-gatherers and horticulturalists bear little resemblance to the pantheistic religions of agricultural societies, and both differ considerably from the monotheistic religions of contemporary Judaism, Islam, or Christianity. Even so, it is possible to identify "religion" in cultures quite distinct from one's own. This suggests that all religions share basic identifying features that distinguish religion, even to an outsider. What are these shared identifying features of religion?

Proximate Mechanisms of Religion

Belief in Supernatural Agents

E. B. Tylor (1871), a founding father of the anthropological study of religion, distilled religion down to a belief in spiritual beings. This definition has had widespread appeal. Tylor noted that supernatural agents are a recurrent and distinguishing feature of religion across widely diverse cultures. These agents share several important features; they are often socially omniscient, powerfully punitive, and empirically unfalsifiable. They vary widely from culture to culture in both the forms they assume and the roles and significance they are accorded.

Cross-cultural studies conducted since the 1950s have repeatedly found a belief in socially omniscient supernatural agents to be common across diverse religious systems (see Johnson 2016:58). These beliefs are not confined to traditional cultures studied by anthropologists; a 2018 survey of Americans conducted by the Pew Forum on Religion and Public Life reported a belief in God or a universal spirit by 80 percent of the US population (Pew Research Center 2018). Cognitive scientists have argued that the supernatural agents of religion, like moving dots on computer screens or faces in the clouds, are simply unintended emanations of cognitive adaptations that have evolved to serve more mundane, survival functions (Atran and Norenzayan 2004:730). Kirkpatrick describes these as a "byproduct of numerous, domain-specific psychological mechanisms that evolved to solve other (mundane) adaptive problems" (Kirkpatrick 1999:921). The universal human propensity to believe in supernatural agents may be a by-product of cognitive mechanisms evolved to deal with very real threats to human survival, such as predation, as proposed by various cognitive scientists (Guthrie 2003). Indeed, religious systems may have co-opted these evolved biases; evolution works on the material at hand. Anthropological and psychological evidence suggests, however, that the supernatural agents of religious belief systems are more than mere by-products (Purzycki and Sosis 2022). They engage our evolved anti-predation cognitive mechanisms, yet they also modify them in socioecologically specific and developmentally patterned ways. Whether supernatural agents are envisioned as totemic spirits, ancestral ghosts, or hierarchical gods is very much dependent upon the socioecological context in which they occur. Yet, regardless of the particular form assumed by the supernatural agents of religion, they are universally "envisioned as possessing knowledge of socially strategic information, having unlimited perceptual access to socially maligned behaviors that occur in private and therefore outside the perceptual boundaries of everyday human agents" (Bering 2005:419).

Research shows a developmental propensity to believe in such socially omniscient supernatural agents. Cross-cultural studies conducted with children between the ages of three and twelve indicate that young children possess an "intuitive theism" (Kelemen 2004:295) that differentiates the social omniscience of supernatural agents from the fallible knowledge of natural social agents. As the child's theory of mind develops, parents and other natural agents are increasingly viewed as limited in their perceptual knowledge; yet, supernatural agents not only remain socially omniscient, but are viewed by children in late childhood as agents capable of acting on such knowledge (Bering 2005; Bering and Bjorklund 2004). Whether these supernatural beings are deemed to be plant or animal spirits, dead ancestors, or powerful gods, they universally know what humans are up to, and they are capable of inflicting supernatural punishment on those who incur their wrath (Alcorta and Sosis 2005:327).

This ontogenetic predisposition to believe in powerful omniscient supernatural beings provides opportunities for the construction of socially relevant moral systems across widely diverse ecologies. Bering (2005:430) asserts "children are simultaneously immersed in unique cultural environments where morality is chiefly determined by socioecological conditions. Although there is likely a common 'moral grammar' underlying all children's development in this domain, the moral particulates of any given society are given shape by the demands of local environments." Atran (2002:278–279) also acknowledges religion's use of supernatural agents in "maintaining the cooperative trust of actors and the trustworthiness of communication by sanctifying the actual order of mutual understandings and social relations." Evolutionary biologist and political scientist Dominic Johnson maintains that this social omniscience and the ability of supernatural agents to mete out very real punishment, including illness, misfortune, and death, ensures social cooperation. Johnson deems these beliefs essential to religion: "Without supernatural consequences, good or bad, religion falls apart" (Johnson 2016:12).

It is clear, however, that a predisposition to believe in supernatural agents is, by itself, incapable of "sanctifying the actual order of mutual understandings and social relations" (Atran 2002:278), as illustrated by the imaginary friends, unseen specters, and intergalactic aliens that populate the world of many children and adults alike. It is possible to be cognizant of religious beliefs without subscribing to them, as any schoolchild who has ever studied Greek mythology can attest. Counterintuitive elements of religious beliefs which render them highly memorable also make them particularly difficult to rationally embrace. Totemic snakes, chimeric gods, and virgin births engage our attention precisely *because* they are counterintuitive. How, then, do such beliefs become sacred truths with the power to influence individual judgment, guide choices and decisions, and motivate selfless behaviors required for social cooperation?

Separation of the Sacred and the Profane

Participation in religious ritual is universally the portal for accessing the mysterious, the sacred, and the divine. Religious ritual does not merely access the sacred, however; it *creates* it (Rappaport 1999:3). Holy water is not simply water that has been discovered to be holy or water that has been rationally demonstrated to have special qualities. It is, rather, water that has been transformed through ritual. For adherents who have participated in sanctifying rituals, the cognitive schema associated with sacred things differs from that of the profane. For Christians, profane water is defined by chemical structure and mundane uses; holy water, however, is set apart from the mundane and instead evokes associations of baptismal rites and spiritual cleansing. The emotional significance of holy and profane water is quite distinct. Not only is it inappropriate to treat holy water as one treats profane water; it is emotionally repugnant. Sacred and profane things are cognitively distinguished by adherents. The critical distinction between them, however, is the emotional significance of sacred things. It is this emotional valancing that transforms ordinary symbols and profane objects into sacred things (Alcorta and Sosis 2005:332).

The concept of the sacred is a universal component of religious systems. Rappaport observes that it is "the domain of the Holy, the constituents of which include the sacred, the numinous, the occult and the divine" (1999:23) that differentiate religious and secular realms. These attributes of religion are mysterious and awesome; they cannot be verbally described or rationally explained, nor can they be comprehended through ordinary modes of perception. By their very nature, they preclude the conscious, task-specific, language-based predispositions of left-hemisphere processing; they derive "their orders of meaning from the non-semantic" (1999:23). It is through participation in communal ritual that these domains are accessed and their orders of meaning perceived.

Communal Ritual: The Root of Religion

Rappaport has called ritual "the ground from which religion grows" (1999:26). It is among the most identifiable elements of religion cross-culturally and can be recognized even when the settings, language, and embedded symbols are unfamiliar. No one would mistake the *molimo* ritual of the Ituri Mbuti of Africa for a Protestant church service, yet both share an underlying structure that differentiates them from ordinary profane behaviors and distinguishes them as religious.

Ritual is not exclusive to religion, nor even to our species. We engage in a multitude of rituals individually and socially every day. Greeting and dating rituals, classroom and workplace rituals, sports and life event rituals all serve to structure social interactions and allow us to accurately predict and appropriately respond to the behavior of others. As among nonhuman animals, human rituals facilitate social interactions and reduce stress, particularly in novel or changing environments. From simple ontogenetic signals such as a bowed head of deference to highly elaborate and increasingly costly rituals such as the patriotic ceremonies and parades of nation-states, ritual serves to structure and facilitate social communication and interaction.

Like the ritualized displays of nonhuman species, costly human rituals exhibit an underlying structure of formality, pattern, sequence, and repetition that serves to arouse and focus attention, heighten awareness, elicit associations, and enhance memory. They also incorporate emotionally evocative innate and ontogenetic signals. The cost-liest human rituals, however, differ from the ritualized displays of nonhuman species in two important ways. Unlike the predominantly dyadic displays of nonhuman species, the costliest human rituals are communal. Some, such as the religious ritual of prayer, may be privately enacted. Yet even such privately enacted human rituals derive from and are learned through participation in communal ritual and are directed toward group symbols and communally sanctified beliefs. The second critical element distinguishing costly human rituals from those of non-human species is the incorporation of abstract symbols. While innate and ontogenetic signals embedded in ritual elicit behavioral responses across all species, only human ritual additionally incorporates *abstract symbols* that are culturally created. When imbued with emotional significance through participation in costly communal ritual, these symbols identify and define social groups; create behavioral norms, influence social judgment, and impact individual behavior (Alcorta and Sosis 2005:331–332).

Religious rituals are among the costliest of human rituals. Across cultures, religious ritual has traditionally been the universal mechanism by which social symbols are transmitted and imbued with emotional meaning and motivational force. Rappaport (1999), Wallace (1966), Eller (2010), and others (Alcorta and Sosis 2005) have argued that it is, specifically, the "doing" of ritual that creates a sense of the sacred and inculcates religious belief. The creation of communal symbols from abstractions, and the imbuing of such symbols with attributions of "awe," "purity," and "danger" are consistent and critical features of religious ritual everywhere (Alcorta and Sosis 2005:332). Rappaport notes that ritual is "the form of action in which those constituents are generated" (1999:23). How does participation in religious ritual accomplish this?

The Biology of Religious Ritual

Religious rituals are biologically significant events. Religious ascetics have long employed isolation, fasting, and pain as doorways to the numinous and divine, while ritual chanting, music, and dance are widespread means to induce euphoria, ecstasy, and trance. Religious rituals vary greatly within and across religious systems, yet all impact both autonomic and neurophysiological systems. The focused meditation of Buddhist monks bears little outward resemblance to the whirling ecstasy of Sufi dervishes. Both, however, induce changes in heart and pulse rate, skin conductance, neuroendocrine levels, and other autonomic functions (Austin 1998; Krumhansl 1997). Neuroimaging studies of practiced meditators reveal structural connectome changes in various brain structures during meditation (Sharp et al. 2018) as well as decreases in default mode network (DMN) activity (Garrison et al. 2015:712). Recent neuroimaging studies of an experienced Mongolian shaman during trance demonstrate alterations in neural networks also (Flor-Henry et al. 2017).

Anthropologists have long puzzled over the seeming irrationality of religious ritual's strict adherence to "form" in the absence of any tangible result. Yet, it is the correct performance of ritual rather than an explicit outcome that is deemed central to its efficacy. The event segmentation of ritual renders ritual events more memorable than non-ritualized contexts. Its "predefined sequences characterized by rigidity, formality, and repetition" (Hobson et al. 2018:261), are cognitively demanding and externally cued. These features of ritual may attenuate activity in the brain's DMN; neuroimaging studies have shown DMN activity to be "attenuated during cognitively demanding, externally-cued tasks" (Greicius et al. 2008:839). Practiced meditators exhibit decreases in DMN activity during meditation (Garrison et al. 2015:712), as do psychoactive substance users, who subjectively report experiences of ineffability, a sense of the numinous, "Oneness," and the divine in association with DMN attenuation (Lebedev et al. 2015; Pollan 2018:305). The DMN has been described as the biological basis of Freud's "ego," as well as the neural basis of "the conscious self" (Carhart-Harris and Friston 2010). Attenuation of DMN activity during religious ritual may contribute to a sense of "communitas" among participants, as well as experiences of "oneness" and ineffability. When associated with religious symbols and beliefs these same attributes of ineffability, numinosity, and the infinite may be conferred upon the symbols and beliefs themselves. Music, another recurrent feature of religious ritual, may further enhance these perceptions.

Music is a central element of religious ritual throughout the world. Music acoustically instantiates ritual's formality, sequence, pattern, and repetition. It further amplifies and intensifies these elements through the use of "rhythmic drivers," such as drumming, chanting, and dance. Described by anthropologist Maurice Bloch as one of the "distinguishing marks of ritual" (1989:21), music is a recurrent and important component of religious ritual across widely diverse cultures and remains a key consistent feature even in the most ritually constrained religions (Alcorta and Sosis 2005:336). Bloch derived his "distinguishing marks of ritual" from ethnographies of traditional societies. A survey of US congregations conducted by Chaves and colleagues (1999:471), however, found music to be the single most consistent feature of contemporary US religious services across congregations, as well.

Music has documented neurophysiological effects on both individual neurophysiology and group behaviors. As a "rhythmic driver," it impacts autonomic functions (Krumhansl 1997:336) and synchronizes "internal biophysiological oscillators to external auditory rhythms" (Scherer and Zentner 2001:372). The coupling of respiration, heart rate, and other body rhythms to these drivers affects a wide array of physiological processes, including brain wave patterns, pulse, and diastolic blood pressure. The ability of music to "couple" or "entrain" participants (Clayton et al. 2020) is present in humans at a very early age (Scherer and Zentner 2001:367). Levenson (2003:348) has shown that synchronized autonomic functions, including such things as pulse rate, heart contractility, and skin conductance, are positively and significantly associated with measures of empathy. The capacity of music to alter skin temperature, muscle tension, cardiovascular function, respiration, norepinephrine, and brain wave patterns all have subjectively reported "emotion inducing effects" (Hirokawa and Ohira 2003:189).

Music has also been shown to increase production of the brain's "feel good" neurochemicals including dopamine, oxytocin, prolactin, and endogeneous opiods (Levitin 2008). These neurochemicals elicit affiliative behaviors and promote social bonding (Carter 1998; Uvnas-Mohlberg 1998). Oxytocin release has been associated with increased in-group affiliation, cooperation, and trust as well as greater out-group hostility (Kosfeld et al. 2005). Oxytocin increases social memory, as well (Rimmele et al. 2009). Prolactin, which has been shown to increase during meditation, is also associated with decreased fearfulness and reduced cortisol concentrations. Dopamine, an inhibitory neurotransmitter that plays a critical role in the brain's reward system, is central to incentive learning, planning, and risk-based decision-making (Dehaene and Changeux 2000; St. Onge and Floresco 2008). Since dopamine elicits positive emotions, stimuli that increase dopamine production are valued. Some stimuli, such as food and music, have inherent reward value; we are born with an innate dopamine response to these things. Other stimuli that have no inherent reward value may attain such value when repeatedly paired with another stimulus that elicits a dopamine response. Once learned, the secondary stimulus also acquires incentive value and can subsequently influence our judgments and behavioral choices (Dehaene and Changeux 2000). The music, movement, and communal ritual of religion activate inherent dopamine responses while associating such responses with social and symbolic stimuli. As a result, the social tenets and sacred symbols of religion acquire incentive value, thereby influencing our subsequent social judgments and behavioral choices (Alcorta and Sosis 2005:337).

The capacity of music to entrain autonomic states, evoke congruent emotions, elicit empathy in listeners, and promote both cooperation and reinforcement learning provides the basis for creating and synchronizing motivational states in ritual participants and associating those states with social symbols (Alcorta and Sosis 2005:337). Recent experiments conducted by a wide array of researchers have found that synchronization of body movements through rhythmic drivers such as music increases group affiliation (Hove and Risen 2009:949), enhances cooperation (Wiltermuth and Heath 2009:1), and improves group performance (Davis et al. 2015). Drawing on research conducted by Fischer and colleagues (2013:115), psychologist Nicholas Hobson and associates sum up this research with the following observation: "Group rituals that involve more synchronous body movements are associated with more trust, cooperation, and feelings of oneness than are other group rituals" (2018:271). The universality of music across religious ritual is likely a major factor in religion's ability to achieve these myriad effects.

Negative Elements of Religious Ritual

Many components of religious ritual induce positive emotional responses, yet there are numerous elements that evoke fear, pain, and terror. Many ritual settings, including shadowed groves, dark caves, and candlelit cathedrals, arouse vigilance by altering sensory perception through unpredictable illumination. Grotesque masks, bleeding statues, and terrible images prominent in many religious rituals engage innate "agency" modules that evoke emotions evolved for response to danger and threat. Physical and mental ordeals inflict pain and suffering, as do self-mortification practices across religions. Terrifying and vengeful gods and demons mete out punishment and demand costly sacrifices. Negative stimuli such as these are central elements of many religious systems. In contrast to the positive affect induced by ecstatic religious ritual, these threatening, fear-inducing, and painful ritual practices evoke intense negative emotions. Such emotions are both motivationally powerful (Vaish et al. 2008) and impossible to forget (Alcorta and Sosis 2005:338).

The Ritual Spectrum and Modes of Religiosity

Not all religious rituals are alike, nor are all equally efficacious in engendering faith communities or imbuing religious symbols with socio-emotional significance and motivational force. Whitehouse's (2004) imagistic and doctrinal "modes of religiosity" aptly describe opposing endpoints of the religious ritual spectrum. The doctrinal mode, familiar to most adherents of contemporary world religions, is one end of this spectrum and is typified by ritual that is recurrent, repetitive, and relatively low arousal. Language-based symbolic systems and positive affect engage predominantly left-hemisphere language and dopaminergic processes. Music and movement are relatively constrained, and social interactions promoted are inclusive in nature.

At the opposite end of the religious ritual spectrum is Whitehouse's "imagistic" mode. The highly intense rituals of the "imagistic" mode are infrequent but emotionally compelling and autonomically arousing. Adolescent initiation rites that subject initiates to a myriad of psychological and physical ordeals typify the imagistic mode. Initiation rites occur only once in an individual's lifetime, but they have long-lasting neurophysiological impacts, particularly when experienced during the brain changes that occur during adolescence (Alcorta 2021).

Both modes of religiosity have autonomic and neurophysiological effects. The language/symbolic/positive affect elements of the doctrinal mode can be expected to preferentially activate predominantly left-hemisphere processes, while the imagistic mode engages the noradrenergic attentional-vigilance systems of the right hemisphere. However, even the least arousing doctrinal religions involve right-hemisphere ritual processes, and the most extreme imagistic religions incorporate left-hemisphere symbolic processes, as well, with most religions falling somewhere between these two extremes (Alcorta 2019).

Religion, Emotion, Belief, and Behavior

The critical role of emotion in religion has long been recognized by scholars. Various psychologists and theologians including William James have emphasized the transcendent, noetic, and numinous elements of religion. The German philosopher Rudolf Otto (1923) described religious emotion as "mysterium tremendum," inspiring awe and dread. For these theorists, it is the emotionally compelling, mystical elements of religion that distinguish it from secular life, separating the sacred from the profane. Not all religions emphasize these elements nor do all religious adherents experience mystical and emotionally transformative feelings. And, as with supernatural beliefs, emotionally compelling and transcendent experiences are not specific to religion. Music, sunsets, and nature may all elicit feelings of awe and numinosity, as may the use of entheogens and temporal lobe epilepsy (Saver and Rabin 1997:498). Mystical, emotive, and transcendent experiences comprise important elements of religion for many but, "even William James, a defender of religion, had to admit that there is nothing essentially religious about religious emotions" (Eller 2010:51).

Even so, as religious historian John Corrigan notes, "There is unmistakably, a tradition of inquiry into the place of emotion in religion that is represented, in the West, in a wide range of figures, from mystics to psychologists, theologians to artists, scriptural exegetes to literary and social structuralists and poststructuralists" (2004:5). Insight into why emotion may be a pivotal element in religion is offered by anthropologists Catherine Lutz and Geoffrey White who deem religious emotions to be "a primary idiom for defining and negotiating social relations of the self in a moral order" (1986:417).

Over the past several decades an extensive scientific literature has accumulated that demonstrates a significant influence of emotions on social judgment, moral choices, and individual behavior. Neuroimaging data have revealed that many, if not most of our decisions and actions are initiated on a subconscious level long before our conscious cognition justifies our choices (Pessiglione et al. 2008:561; van Gaal and Lamme 2012:287). Intense emotions etch subconscious emotional memories that are nearly impossible to erase (LeDoux 1996). Emotions impact both our memories and our sense of time (Dawson and Sleek 2018; Dolcos et al. 2017). Since episodic memory is intimately integrated with our perceptions of time and space, attenuation of our episodic memory during intensely emotional religious experiences may additionally confer attributes of timelessness, the infinite, and the eternal upon ritual and its associated symbols. Anthropologist Tanya Luhrmann's description of an evangelical conversion experience suggests this phenomenon: "(H)e felt electricity in his body; he shook; he spoke in tongues; time crawled to a stop – in a classic Holy Spirit experience within evangelical Protestantism" (2012:146).

Those who deem the emotive rituals, counterintuitive beliefs, and supernatural agents of religion to be mere by-products of "useful" cognitive adaptations miss the point. It is *precisely* the emotionally evocative rituals, attention-arresting narratives, and bigger than life, all-knowing supernatural agents of religion that engage our vigilance and threat systems, evoke powerful sensory and somatic responses, and create the neurophysiological conditions for associating these somatic and emotional responses with the socially relevant symbols and schema of religious systems.

Ritual, Emotion, and the Sacred

The ability of religious ritual to elicit both positive and negative emotional responses in participants provides a mechanism for the creation of motivationally powerful communal symbols. Emotionally evocative elements of religious ritual prime ritual participants for associating socially salient symbols and beliefs with evoked emotions through both conditioning and reinforcement learning (Daw 2007:1505). These processes engage brain structures in limbic and prefrontal regions of the brain that emotionally "weight" stimuli, thereby influencing subsequent social judgments and behaviors. The OFC, the prefrontal region previously noted as critical for "top-down" control of reactive aggression (see Section 2), is central to this process (Blair and Charney 2003). The use of emotionally evocative elements of religious ritual to "weight" social symbols and beliefs through associational learning provides a means of creating common group motivators and influencing individual choices and behaviors. The "ecstasy" experienced through the music and movement of Sufi dancing may, thus, positively valence the religious poetry with which it is associated. Likewise, ingestion of peyote by the Huichol Indians with its potentiation of the dopaminergic reward system provides a neurophysiological basis for investing the communal Peyote Hunt itself with sacred significance (Myerhoff 1974). Negative emotional responses elicited by shadowed cathedrals, fearsome masks, and painful ordeals are also powerful for investing the supernatural agents of religious systems with awesome, terrible, and extraordinary power, as well. Such symbols are not inherently pleasurable, but they are motivationally powerful, prompting "avoidance of violations of social norms" (Blair and Charney 2003:26).

Participation in communal religious rituals provides a mechanism for investing previously neutral stimuli with deep emotional significance capable of influencing judgments, motivating behavior, subordinating individual self-interest to the collective needs of the larger group, and creating cohesive, cooperative social groups (Alcorta and Sosis 2005:338–339).

Religious Ritual, Commitment, and Identity

The symbolic and metaphorical nature of religious ritual engages broad associational networks, with emotionally evocative elements of ritual investing these components with heightened significance and meaning through both conditioning and reinforcement learning. Participation in religious ritual is also a powerful public signal of belief, commitment, and acceptance (Bulbulia and Sosis 2011; Sosis 2006). Ritual participation identifies group membership and declares acceptance of group relationships, values, and norms. In so doing, it defines the social and moral order and establishes the individual's identity within it. This clarification of social relationships and expected behaviors reduces ambiguity and uncertainty in social interactions, thereby reducing stress.

Cross-cultural and experimental studies have shown that participation in communal religious ritual is significantly and positively associated with reduced stress and anxiety (Alcorta 2016; Koenig 2008; Sosis and

Handwerker 2011). Religious participation extends both individual (McCullough et al. 2000:211) and group longevity (Sosis and Bressler 2003:211) and enhances in-group social cooperation (Sosis and Ruffle 2004:87). Religious ritual creates and reinforces in- and out-group identities, with powerful consequences for individual behavior. Considerable research shows a strong human propensity to create such groups, as well as a propensity to reify one's own group to the detriment of others (Eller 2010). The ability of religious ritual to symbolize and sanctify unfalsifiable, timeless truths and invest them with emotional salience and motivational force is central to its ultimate purpose – the creation of cohesive, cooperative social groups.

Ultimate Function of Religion

This discussion underscores the fact that religion cannot be defined by any single feature. It encompasses numerous elements, including belief in supernatural agents, concepts of the sacred, and communal ritual. These and the other proximate mechanisms of religion bolster Eller's contention that "religion is not a thing but rather a composite" (2010:51). More than a century ago Emile Durkheim proposed a definition of religion that recognizes both the complexity and cross-cultural diversity of religion; it also suggests the ultimate function of religion. Durkheim's studies of Australian totemic religions led him to reject a singular definition of religion as an ideology, a collection of rituals, ecstatic experiences, or supernatural beliefs. He instead proposed that religion is "a unified system of beliefs and practices relative to sacred things, that is to say set apart and forbidden, beliefs and practices which unite into one single moral community, called a church, all those who adhere to them" (1954 [1915]:47).

Supernatural beliefs, emotionally evocative experiences, concepts of the sacred and profane, and symbolic, communal ritual are all distinguishing core features of religion. Yet, religion also incorporates myth, meaning, authority, moral obligation, and taboo (Sosis 2020:142). The specific configuration of these various elements, as well as their interrelationship and relative importance, vary from culture to culture and over time. Some cultures, such as the Hua of Papua, New Guinea, have few if any beliefs in supernatural agents. Their religious system primarily involves rituals and taboos surrounding food and sex and emphasizes sanctity and myth. In contrast, the Kwaio, whose religion centers on belief in ancestral spirits, have no myths regarding their own origins, but rather myths related to the origins of their rituals. In contrast, the Ilahita Arapesh are "so enveloped in myth that the arrival of an anthropologist was perceived as a fulfilled mythic prophecy" (Sosis 2020:147–148). Some cultures, such as the Yaghan of Patagonia and the Ache of Paraguay practice few communal rituals, instead emphasizing the oral transmission of sacred knowledge. Others, such as the Ndembu of Africa, expend much time, energy, and resources on communal ritual, particularly prolonged and painful adolescent rites of passage. All these religious systems incorporate basic elements of religion, yet the configuration and integration of these elements are as varied as the cultures which practice them. What drives such differences across religious systems, and why does the costliness of these systems vary so widely?

Behavioral Ecology and Religion

Over the past three decades, human behavioral ecologists have applied the theoretical perspective and methodological tools of animal behavioral ecology to the study of religion (Sosis and Bulbulia 2011:343). One recent development in this work is to approach religion as a complex adaptive system composed of dynamically interacting components which function together to address socioecological challenges through enhanced social cooperation (Sosis 2019). This approach posits that religious systems incorporate core elements, including authority, meaning, moral obligation, myth, ritual, the sacred, supernatural agents, and taboo, in a configuration that addresses the specific socioecological needs of a particular society. While the core structure of religious systems consists of interactions between these eight elements, all elements may not interact directly, although they do all interact with and through ritual, which comprises the heart of religious systems (Sosis 2020:144).

From birth to death, humans live in groups. Like the troops of our cousins, the chimpanzees and bonobos, human groups afford vigilance and protection from predators, expanded breeding opportunities, alloparenting assistance, information transfer, and companionship. In contrast to our primate cousins, humans also depend on social groups for food acquisition, processing, and distribution. From the collective hunting and gathering of our earliest human ancestors to the communal processing and cooking of food, to the highly distributed and intricately integrated food production networks of today, human social cooperation has been critical to our species' ability to acquire, protect, and process the basic resources upon which we all depend. These benefits of sociality enhance the fitness of individuals within the group.

Yet, social groups also introduce new problems of competition, free-loading, and possible defection (Krebs and Dawkins 1984:120–133). These problems escalate as group size increases and genetic relatedness among group members decreases (Alcorta and Sosis 2013:586). Different species have met these challenges in various ways. Highly cooperative eusocial insects, such as bees and ants, live in closely related kin groups of task-structured castes, thereby ensuring that cooperative behaviors are coordinated and all group members benefit through inclusive fitness. Numerous other social species benefit from inclusive fitness through groups composed of kin-related individuals, as well. Within such groups, dominance hierarchies structure social relations and control intragroup competition by regulating access to mates and resources. Some animals, such as bats living in colonies that include nonkin, employ a "tit for tat" strategy of sharing resources with trusted "friends." While this reciprocal altruism extends cooperation to unrelated individuals, it necessarily confines the extent of cooperative interactions to familiar conspecifics whose behavior can be remembered and accurately predicted.

Human social groups incorporate all these strategies. When social groups are small and closely related, competition and collective action problems are relatively limited by the operation of kin selection and reciprocity. Informal social hierarchies and divisions of labor within the group serve to regulate resource access and minimize competition. As groups grow larger and genetic relatedness decreases, however, there is increasing incentive for individuals to free ride on the efforts of others. Under these circumstances, group members who can benefit from the cooperative efforts of others with no costs to themselves realize the greatest gains. While everyone may gain if all group members invest in the cooperative goal, attaining such cooperation is often difficult without mechanisms that limit the ability of some group members to free ride on the efforts of others. As the risks associated with cooperative endeavors increase and probabilities of detection decrease, there is greater incentive for individuals to defect and free ride. As a result, whenever an individual can falsely claim cooperation and then successfully defect, the most credible signals of cooperative intentions are those that entail costs and are difficult to fake (Alcorta and Sosis 2013:586).

Across time and space, human societies have differed widely, as evidenced by the diversity of subsistence strategies, social organization, and ecologies throughout history and across cultures. The social and collective action challenges confronted by small-scale, fission–fusion societies of nomadic hunter-gatherers differ greatly from those faced by semisedentary horticulturalists, migratory pastoralists, intensive agriculturalists, or large-scale industrial and commercial societies. Yet, across all these subsistence types, those societies most able to successfully resolve collective action problems, such as resource overexploitation, defection, freeloading, and defense reap the greater benefits achieved through cooperative action.

For evolutionary anthropologists, the ultimate purpose of religion is enhancement of social cooperation and coordination. These researchers assert that religion has evolved as an adaptive system to address human collective action problems. If so, it is likely that religious systems and the costliness of associated religious behaviors and practices vary cross-culturally in relation to the benefits to be derived from social cooperation within given social and ecological circumstances. The costliest religious systems would be expected to occur in those societies facing the greatest collective challenges. A cross-cultural comparison of subsistence strategies, socioecologies, and religious systems appears to support this expectation.

5 Cooperation and Conflict

More than half a century ago anthropologist Anthony Wallace (1966) proposed a fourfold typology of religion including shamanic, communal, Olympian, and monotheistic religions. He viewed these religion "types" as cumulative; societies with communal institutions also incorporated shamanic institutions, Olympian religions incorporated both shamanic and communal institutions, while monotheistic religions incorporated all types. Wallace's typology significantly simplifies both the reality and the complexity of religious systems. Few religious systems fit neatly into Wallace's "types." Moreover, a linear progression of social, cultural, and religious systems has been long discredited, as well. Wallace's typology is, however, a useful heuristic tool for identifying proximate mechanisms of religion – core components that underlie "how" religion promotes social cooperation. Wallace's typology also suggests "why" religion works and helps distinguish the ultimate causes that drive both the costs and adaptive success of religious systems across diverse socioecologies.

Shamanic Religions

Wallace's first religion type is shamanic religion. Shamanic religions, in general, most frequently occur in relatively egalitarian hunter-gatherer and small-scale horticultural societies. Reflecting the socioecological concerns of these societies, shamanic religions are largely animistic. High gods – single, all-powerful creator dieties – with limited or no involvement in human daily life exist in some shamanic religions but are absent in others. The shamanic world is populated by spirits, including animal and human souls, as well as local spirits capable of wreaking havoc on human enterprises. These spirits must, therefore, be acknowledged and propitiated. It is the role of the shaman to regulate relations between the human and spirit worlds, particularly in relation to resources and illness. The shaman holds no formal authority within these small-scale, kin-based egalitarian societies. It is instead the shaman's ability to effectively communicate with the spirit world that affords him/her the moral authority to impose taboos, address violations of communal ritual regulations, and publicly identify transgressors.

Shamanic journeys to the spirit world are dangerous undertakings. Novices frequently serve lengthy apprenticeships under an experienced shaman to learn how to properly journey to and safely communicate with the spirit world. The demands of shamanic training and trancing are intense, and the shamanic trance is exhausting. Entering the spirit world is both a perilous and ecstatic experience (Winkelman 2000). Fasting, dancing, self-mortification, entheogen use, and other psychologically and physically demanding practices are required to enter the spirit world through the portal of shamanic trance (Winkelman 1986). The specific spirits of shamanic religions differ widely from group to group and reflect local socio-ecologies. For example, among the Inuit of the circumpolar regions, Sedna, the Keeper of the Sea Animals, is an important spirit who must be visited annually by the shaman to request the release of the game from her domain to ensure human resources for the coming year (Wallace 1966:90). Shamans may also visit the spirit world in the event of illness within the group, during times of stress, or at the request of an individual.

Shamanic religions impose relatively low costs on social groups. Recurring communal rituals that consume time, energy, and resources are minimized, with the shaman conducting rituals primarily on an "as needed" basis in response to illness, misfortune, or stress. In the absence of formal political systems, shamanic religions informally regulate social interaction and promote cooperation. By invoking a socially and ecologically relevant spirit world that is socially omniscient, punitively powerful, and empirically unfalsifiable, shamanic religions provide a relatively low-cost solution to the collective action problems of social compliance and cooperation in small egalitarian fission–fusion societies.

Communal Religions

The second of Wallace's religious types is communal religions, akin to what sociologist Robert Bellah (2011) has designated "tribal" religions. Wallace viewed communal religions as encompassing magic and ancestral cults, as well as the shamanic cults previously discussed. Trobriand Islanders typified communal religions in Wallace's typology, with elaborate mortuary communal ceremonies, and an ongoing pivotal role of ancestral spirits in the life of the living.

Traditional Trobriand Islanders were a sedentary horticultural society in which land and resources were controlled by matrilineal clans. Communal religions occur across many such prestate clans and lineage-based societies, including pastoralists such as the Nuer of the Sudan

(Evans-Pritchard 1940), as well as among sedentary horticulturalists, including the Ndembu of Africa (Turner 1969), the Ilahita Arapesh of New Guinea (Tuzin 1976), and the Kalapalo of Brazil (Basso 1988). Communal religions also typified the hunter-gatherer cultures of the Pacific Northwest that exploited a resource-rich ecology which permitted the development of large, sedentary societies such as those of the Haida, Kwakiutl, and Tlingit.

Throughout the world, clan and lineage systems, like those of sedentary horticulturalists and pastoralists, regulate and control resource management. These kin-based "corporations" provide a pragmatic solution for defining and controlling property rights and obligations, as well as an inclusive fitness approach to mitigating freeloading and enforcing social control within the lineage unit. Living male elders, and less frequently female elders, serve as "trustees" for the lineage, managing resources and adjudicating lineage disputes on behalf of the ancestral spirits who maintain an active interest in clan affairs. These spirits must be regularly consulted, honored, and propitiated through communal ceremonies that simultaneously serve to communicate and validate clan and lineage membership, authority, and rights within the larger society.

Shamanic cults continue to play an important role in communal religions with shamans continuing to serve as intermediaries with the spirit world. "Dark shamans" also assume a greater role within many such societies as those with lesser political power employ magic, witchcraft, and sorcery as mechanisms for exerting greater social control (Wright 2015). In the absence of a centralized political authority, shamans frequently fulfill other informal political functions, as well, as exemplified by the "leopard skin chief" of the Nuer (Greuel 1971:1115).

In terms of the time, energy, and resources expended by group members, communal religions are costlier than shamanic religions. This is particularly pronounced during periods of social and/or resource stress. Clan and lineage rituals to honor and propitiate ancestors must be regularly performed and life cycle rituals such as adolescent rites of passage assume increased importance, frequency, and costliness. The increased costs of communal religions reflect the expanded social and political roles assumed by religion in these more populous, semi-sedentary, and sedentary societies.

The many rituals, practices, and taboos surrounding ancestral spirits serve important corporate functions for the clan or lineage group, while public rituals simultaneously communicate and regulate group membership and relationships.

Adolescent rites of passage are among the most important rituals of communal religions. These rites are conducted for the explicit purpose of transmitting sacred knowledge from one generation to the next, yet they also serve economic and political functions through their alteration of initiates' roles, statuses, and relationships. Adolescent rites of passage may include a single individual or a group and may be conducted for males, females, or both. In many clan/lineage societies adolescent rites of passage are prolonged and painful ordeals endured by groups of age-graded adolescent males. Following their initiation into adulthood, these males create a standing "warrior" class within the society that crosscuts lineage ties and functions to defend and acquire group resources through intergroup competition and warfare.

Many of the functions of communal religion differ from those of shamanic religions in fission–fusion societies of nomadic hunter-gatherers. Since most social disputes in these latter groups are settled with one's feet, and religious taboos serve primarily to prevent resource overexploitation, the need for recurrent, costly religious practices is diminished. The shift to larger sedentary populations and the need for ongoing resource management, control, and defense introduces new social and political challenges for human groups. The emergence and institutionalization of kin-based clans and lineage systems solved some of these challenges by creating cooperative groups for controlling access to resources and enhancing production. Yet, these groups, too, faced problems of cooperation, integration, and freeloading. The supernatural punishments of religion afforded a parsimonious means to overcome these problems. Evolutionary biologist Dominic Johnson notes "while the types and sources of supernatural punishment vary, what is striking is that they all tend to be means to the same end: the reduction of self-interested behavior and the promotion of cooperation" (2016:86). Participation in communal rituals propitiated ancestral spirits, but also publicly acknowledged lineage elders as representatives of those spirits. These recurrent rituals both communicated and validated lineage identity and property rights while simultaneously fostering group identity and cooperation.

Olympian Religions

Olympian religions comprise the third religious type in Wallace's taxonomy. Olympian religions are typified by the religions of ancient Greece and Rome. They emerged in populous agricultural societies with urban centers, formalized central authority, and a political bureaucracy. While retaining both the shamanic and communal cults previously discussed, Olympian religions incorporate an official "Great Gods" cult, as well, that includes state-authorized priesthoods, temples, rituals, and myths. Olympian religions "maintained an elaborate cult institution centering in the propitiation of a pantheon of several high gods ... (who) ... directly sanctioned the political structure and directly controlled the various departments of nature" (Wallace 1966:99). Their worship required full-time religious specialists and permanent temples under the aegis of the king, who was frequently himself deemed to be divine. Across many Olympian religions, powerful and capricious gods demanded human as well as animal sacrifices, with elaborate, state-sponsored public ceremonies conducted to ensure proper propitiation. Eller notes that "it is in highly formalized political systems – the Greco-Roman states, the Hawaiian and Dahomean kingdoms, and the Mayan and Aztec empires – that we find the most extensive and elaborated sacrificial traditions" (2010:108). The bureaucratic pantheon of gods and goddesses who dabbled in human affairs reflected the socially stratified, pluralistic, and politically centralized societies in which they occurred.

In contrast to the largely ad hoc, local nature of shamanic and communal religions, Olympian religions were multicultural and institutionalized. They amalgamated local beliefs, myths, rituals, and traditions of the empire's diverse populations within a broader, hierarchically structured framework of randomly capricious and punitively powerful anthropomorphic deities. With the emergence of social stratification, political centralization, a priestly class, and the advent of writing, Olympian religions were also increasingly codified. "Slowly, as a body of writings, a *canon*, settled, a single uniform – or at least official – doctrine or dogma took shape" (Eller 2010:67).

Monotheistic Religions

The last religious "type" in Wallace's typology is monotheistic religion. Noting that "no religion is absolutely monotheistic, since other spiritual beings are invariably recognized by a large segment of the population" (Wallace 1966:100), Wallace describes monotheistic religions as "politically established, or at least politically related, ecclesiastical institutions" (Wallace 1966: 100). Monotheistic religions replace "the theological, mythological, and ritual pluralism of Olympian religion with a metaphysically simpler belief in one Supreme Being who either controls the other supernaturals, or expresses himself through them" (Wallace 1966:100). According to Eller, monotheistic religion is "everything that local religions are not" (Eller 2010:69). In contrast to shamanic, communal, and Olympian religions, monotheistic religions are "formal, institutionalized, canonical, universalistic, dualistic, exclusivistic . . . and individualistic" (Eller 2010:69). In contrast to the animism of shamanic religions, the ancestor worship of communal religions, and the pantheism of Olympian religions, the gods of monotheistic religions are believed to be the only one true god by their respective communities. These gods are omnipresent, omniscient, and omnipotent, as well as awesome, terrible, righteous, and moral. Most significantly, monotheistic gods demand morality from their adherents, as well, a morality that may be engendered through love, but enforced through sacrifice, fire, and brimstone.

Wallace's typology of religion provides a useful tool for categorizing widely diverse religious systems. It also suggests that variance across religious systems reflects differences in socioecologies and the collective action problems posed. Having outlined Wallace's typology of religion, we now turn to an analysis of his religious "types" to examine and explain religious diversity and its underlying causes.

What can Wallace's typology tell us about religion? Although this typology fails to capture the considerable cross-cultural diversity and complexity of religious systems, it does provide a useful heuristic tool for examining religious systems as evolved adaptations within specific socioecologies.

Adaptations solve problems that organisms face in their local environment. They evolve through the process of natural selection when a particular trait confers a fitness advantage within a given environment. The beaks of Darwin's finches are the iconic example of this process. The fifteen recognized species of these birds derived from a common ancestor that arrived on the Galapagos Islands approximately 2 million years ago. This original population underwent an adaptive radiation across the archipelago as small groups colonized different ecological niches throughout the islands and began exploiting different resources. Over time, beak sizes and shapes across these populations increasingly diverged as beaks more efficient for exploiting local resources evolved through the process of natural selection

Darwin's finches illustrate the fact that evolved traits are only adaptive in relation to specific ecologies. Evolutionary scientists therefore pay close attention to how variation in ecological conditions can explain variation in traits of interest. Like the beaks of Darwin's finches, the differences across Wallace's four types of religion suggest this same variation. These differences are not random but instead exhibit patterned variation. It is relatively easy to see the adaptive advantage of different beaks for exploiting different food sources. What, however, are the adaptive advantages of different religious systems?

Religion and Social Cooperation

Evolutionary anthropologists consider religion's ability to promote cooperation to be its ultimate evolutionary function (Alcorta and Sosis 2005; Bulbulia and Sosis 2011; Sosis and Alcorta 2003). When individual costs are high, but the potential benefits of cooperation are great, costly religious practices provide a reliable mechanism for minimizing free-riding and maximizing cooperation (Sosis and Alcorta 2003:267). A review of Wallace's religious typology indicates that across cultures the frequency and costliness of sacred rituals performed are correlated with measures of social complexity and reflective of the ecological challenges confronted.

Nomadic Fission–Fusion Societies and Shamanic Religion

Small bands of hunter-gatherers inhabiting severe environments face very different social and ecological challenges than those faced by large sedentary populations of hunters-gatherers in resource-rich environments. These, in turn, both differ from the collective action challenges faced by large agricultural state societies. The fission–fusion social structure of nomadic band societies permits the simple resolution of most social disputes and readjustment of population-resource homeostasis through the redistribution of the human population. Interpersonal disputes, which may be exacerbated by resource depletion, are generally settled by one household or group relocating to a new band. The main collective action challenge confronted by fission–fusion societies is potential overexploitation of scattered common pool resources, such as game populations and waterholes. Such resources cannot be regularly monitored but are vital for group survival.

In these small nomadic fission–fusion societies socially omniscient and potentially punitive animistic and totemic supernatural agents of religion monitor common pool resources. Taboos and practices surrounding the use of such resources are invoked and reinforced through participation in recurrent group rituals during periods of "fusion," and on an "as needed" basis in response to illness, misfortune, and resource stress. These shamanic rituals publicly signal and validate the involvement of supernatural agents in monitoring and enforcing sacred values surrounding common pool resources.

Cross-cultural research on common pool resources across forty-eight indigenous societies throughout the world provides empirical support for this relationship. This research found only "a single case in which people invoked purely secular means for enforcing rules" (Johnson 2016:60). Nearly four-fifths of the societies studied believed that supernaturally imposed material punishments, such as illness, disease, misfortune, or disaster, awaited those who violated social norms surrounding the protection and use of such resources (Johnson 2016:60).

Various researchers have noted a positive relationship between stress levels and the incidence of religious ritual. Victor Turner reported that among the Ndembu "there is a close connection between social conflict and ritual at the levels of village and 'vicinage'" (1969:10). Rappaport also observed that spacing of the ritual kaiko cycles of the Tsembaga Maring was contingent on interhousehold stress levels (1984:154). This triggering of religious ritual by perceived stress provides an important mechanism for calibrating the costs of religion with the need for social compliance and cooperation. In the absence of common pool resource concerns, religious costs may be reduced or absent. Conversely, intensified competition for common pool resources, as occurred among the Arunta and other indigenous cultures of the Australian desert, correlates with an increase in both the practices and costs of religion. Inuit religious taboos regarding game animals served similar functions (Wallace 1966:90), as did the sacred taboos surrounding water holes among the !Kung San of the Kalahari Desert. Across these ecologically and geographically diverse societies, religious beliefs and practices provided a flexibly adaptive system for achieving social cooperation in relation to the exploitation of common pool resources.

Clan and Lineage Systems and Communal Religions

Resource-rich ecologies such as the Pacific northwest coast region allow the development of larger sedentary populations. In such ecologies, the small nomadic fission–fusion bands of nuclear families are replaced by extended clan and lineage groups with vested property rights in group resources. Horticulture and the more populous, sedentary settlements this entails are also accompanied by shifts in social organization that vest increasing economic and political power in extended clan and lineage groups responsible for land control, management, and defense. Ancestral clan and lineage spirits assume greater roles in the religious system and communal rituals increase in frequency and importance. Clan and lineage rites and practices to honor and propitiate these spirits both create and reinforce group identities, including moieties, clans, and lineages. These sacred communal rites also establish and sanctify property rights and obligations across lineages while authorizing the social and political authority of clan and lineage elders.

Increases in the size, permanence, and complexity of tribal prestate societies escalate the challenges of intragroup cooperation and intensify intergroup competition. While the use of corporate lineage groups for controlling key resources solves problems of asset management; it simultaneously introduces novel inter-lineage competition and cooperative challenges. The ability to resolve social conflicts through fission–fusion processes diminishes with increasing lineage control of vital resources and the escalation of intergroup competition and conflict.

In addition to intergroup resource competition and raiding, prestate lineage-based societies faced numerous internal collective action challenges. The authority of male elders within clan and lineage groups served to control and regulate intra-lineage conflict and cooperation. Regulation of inter-lineage relations, however, was more problematic. Segmentary lineage systems, tribal councils of elders, and secret societies that crosscut lineage groups all comprised alternative solutions to this problem. In many societies, Councils of Elders encompassing the heads of lineages within the society emerged to mediate disputes. These Councils enlisted the sanction and aid of the ancestors, accessed through diviners, shamans, and communal rites. Religious specialists were frequently called on to mediate disputes through their ability to communicate with the will of the spirits, as well. Among the pastoral Nuer of Africa the leopard skin "chief" fulfilled this role in the absence of an official political authority (Greuel 1971:1115).

Communal rituals increased in frequency and importance in response to increased socioecological stressors (Hobson et al. 2018:263). In horticultural and pastoral societies facing increased intergroup conflict, raiding, and competition, the composition, form, and function of adolescent rites of passage underwent profound changes, as well. These rites shifted from a recognition of individual female menarche to the creation of age-graded groups of adolescent males who crosscut lineage loyalties and created a standing army of tribal warriors. In the absence of official political authorities and a standing police force, it was the unfalsifiable and socially omniscient supernatural agents of religious systems that promoted social cooperation and compliance through the threat of very material supernatural punishment (Johnson 2016).

In many prestate societies inter-lineage rivalries gave rise to ongoing blood feuds and revenge killings. In the absence of a centralized authority, magic, witchcraft, and sorcery assumed increased importance as mechanisms for resolving disputes, exacting revenge, and exerting political control (Strathern and Stewart 2005; Wright 2015). Societies facing escalating levels of intergroup competition and conflict also confronted additional problems. The need to successfully combat outside groups required an effective warrior group, yet success in intergroup raiding and warfare contributed to increasing internal inequality as lineages of the most successful warriors grew in size, wealth, and power from the seizure of women and resources as the spoils of war. Increasingly violent sacred rites of passage for groups of adolescent boys created the necessary warrior groups in some societies. These terrifying and violent rites forged "bands of brothers" among the future combatants and promoted subordination of self-interest to the needs of the group.

Eller has argued that the shamanic and communal religions of prestate societies "belonged to or applied to one specific group of people as well as to one specific territory" (2010:66). He has described these religions as "ad hoc, noncodified, 'patently social', and concrete" (2010: 67). Some recurrent communal rituals occurred, although most religious rituals were conducted "to deal with specific spiritual or practical problems when they arise" (2010:67). The absence of writing and associated lack of official doctrine in these religious systems preferenced ritual and metaphorical narrative and provided systemic flexibility to meet changing conditions. Increasing inequality, social stratification, and intergroup competition drove pivotal changes in these societies, however, as social, political, and religious systems changed, as well.

Social Stratification, City-States, and Olympian Religions

The emergence of Olympian religions across numerous geographic and cultural regions suggests that this religious "type" was an adaptive response to the challenges of social control and cooperation faced by increasingly large and diverse societies experiencing escalating internal and external conflict. The shift to intensive agriculture and the concomitant development of large, sedentary populations of socially stratified groups triggered significant changes in both political and religious systems. Formalization of political authority was supported by the institutionalization of religion. In addition to the natural and ancestral spirits of prestate societies, a pantheon of omniscient and powerful gods and goddesses emerged, reflecting both the uncontrollable natural forces impacting agriculture and daily life and the ongoing diversity of cultures subsumed by growing state civilizations. These Olympian religions "maintained an elaborate cult institution centering in the propitiation of a pantheon of several high gods ... (who) ... directly sanctioned the political structure and directly controlled the various departments of nature" (Wallace 1966:99).

Shamanic and communal rituals of individuals, families, and lineages continued to be practiced alongside costly state rituals that reinforced the political order by integrating diverse groups and fostering compliance to a reified political elite. Ritual sacrifice, both animal and human, comprised a central component of public ceremonies in Olympian societies across the globe. Such public sacrifice viscerally signaled the power of the king as arbiter of life and death in service to the gods, with victims including rulers of defeated enemies (Eller 2010:381). While victims were predominantly members of "out-groups," including war captives and enslaved individuals from competing societies, human sacrifice sometimes included the relatively powerless within the society as well, particularly orphans, women, and children (Eller 2010:103).

In traditional Hawaiian society, the king was the "supreme sacrificer," a role which "gives him authority over men, since it makes his actions more perfect and efficacious than theirs" (Valeri 1985:140–142). In the African kingdom of Dahomey human sacrifice was ubiquitous; it occurred in response to the daily awakening of the king, the building of his palace, during ancestral rituals, as a prelude to war, and upon the king's death among other events (Eller 2010:102). Egyptian pharaohs and Chinese emperors alike were accompanied in death by entombed wives and members of their retinue. Pre-Christian European societies from Vikings to Gauls to Greeks conducted gruesome sacrificial rites, including drowning with rocks, crushing under the keels of ships, burning alive, and dismembering. Romans fed Christians to the lions. The spectacle of human sacrifice that typified public religious ceremonies in Mayan and Aztec societies was even more gruesome and elaborate, fully embodying the power of the king as arbiter of life and death in service to the gods. Animal and especially human sacrifice served to appease and propitiate capricious and bloodthirsty gods. Across these geographically diverse cultures, ritual sacrifice sent a singular and clear message to friends and enemies alike; powerful kings, like the omnipotent gods they served, were not to be denied.

Empires and the Moralizing Gods of Monotheism

The ongoing growth of powerful city-states and the emergence of complex multistate empires encompassing numerous cultures and socio-ecologies introduced new collective action problems. As city-states grew into empires through increased agricultural productivity and the ongoing subjugation of groups defeated in warfare, the rulers of these complex, socially stratified societies amassed ever larger armies, both to conquer out-groups and control increasingly diverse groups within. Religion remained a critical element in lowering the costs of maintaining social cohesion and promoting in-group cooperation, and sacrifice became an increasingly prominent element of communal ritual. Many rulers were themselves viewed as deities, and even those not perceived to be personally divine enjoyed the benefits of sacred privilege supported by a specialized priestly class that controlled religious ritual, doctrine, and practices.

Ongoing military conquests transformed many city-states into far-flung empires. These empires incorporated multiple ethnicities and religions and frequently spanned large geographic regions. The ongoing control, defense, and administration of these regions introduced new challenges. Central among these was the need for achieving social cooperation and compliance across disparate cultures. Military occupation afforded both a potent signal and purveyor of violence for most empires but exacted a high cost. Moreover, as empires expanded, the need to continuously add new military recruits entailed the use of captured slaves as well as conscripted soldiers across religious, ethnic, and social groups. Forging cohesive and committed fighting units from these diverse populations was essential for preventing desertion and mutiny, as well as for ensuring effective military control.

The Roman Empire illustrates these challenges. The Romans maintained both extensive bureaucracies and large standing armies to ensure compliance from those they ruled, but they also faced significant challenges in monitoring and enforcing such compliance owing to social inequality, cultural diversity, and the expansive geographic distances involved. Numerous benefits accrued to those included in the Roman Empire including technologically advanced infrastructure and extensive trade networks that provided a plethora of essential and exotic goods. Urban centers and the maintenance of peace through the Pax Romana brought additional benefits to Roman citizens. Across much of the Empire these benefits were sufficient to quell dissent and insure integration of subjected populations. Johnson (2016:184) has compellingly argued that concepts of civic duty and material advantages provided by inclusion in the Roman Empire were unique in their ability to expand and sustain the empire in the absence of an encompassing and unifying religion. Yet Rome's extensive network of well-engineered roads and aqueducts, its vibrant cities, and its Pax Romana depended upon a well-disciplined and technologically advanced military who constructed and maintained the empire's infrastructure and who secured peace through both a powerful signal of force as well as its violent execution. While the eyes of Roman gods may not have been watching the far-flung subjects of the Roman Empire, the eyes of insurrectionists whose heads adorned Roman pikes throughout the empire certainly did. Expansion of the empire resulted in an increasingly diverse military that included both captured slaves and ethnically diverse conscripts. Over time, the escalating costs of empire maintenance were increasingly offset by the erosion of pay and benefits provided to the military. Internal insurrections grew, fueling the fires for external invasions. By the fourth century AD, the need to cohesify and unite the fragmented and disaffected Roman military was acute.

The shift from the polytheistic state religion of Rome to monotheistic Christianity initiated by Constantine in the fourth century likely derived from this need (Drake 2005). Historical records indicate that Constantine's adoption of Christianity was initiated by a dream (or vision) in which he was advised "to mark the heavenly sign of God on the shields of his soldiers and then engage in battle. He did as he was commanded and by means of a slanted letter X with the top of its head bent round, he marked Christ on their shields" (Drake 2005:113). Constantine's subsequent defeat of Maxentius, his contender for the imperial throne, and his legalization of Christianity throughout the Roman Empire paved the way for monotheism with the adoption of Christianity as the official Roman state religion in 380 AD.

Constantine's use of religion to successfully unite his troops and his empire was not original. His use of a specifically monotheistic Christian symbol acknowledged the pragmatic need to unite an ethnically diverse, socially disparate, and economically depressed military into a cohesively united and morally committed force. More importantly, it signaled a shift from the syncretic polytheism of the Roman state to a moralistic monotheism that accepted all social classes and ethnicities but whose omniscient, omnipotent, omnipresent god demanded exclusivity in return. Constantine's success over Maxentius was but the first of many subsequent Holy Wars fought under the Christian banner.

Like the emperor himself, the one true god of monotheistic religions is omnipotent, vengeful, and jealous. He is also socially omniscient and demanding of moral righteousness in his adherents. For the very mortal rulers of large scale, far-flung empires characterized by great cultural diversity and tremendous social inequality, the righteous morality of the omniscient, omnipotent, omnipresent gods of monotheistic religions affords an ever-present means of eliciting social compliance and cooperation.

Is there any empirical evidence that the moralizing gods of monotheism achieve such cooperation and compliance? A considerable amount of cross-cultural research has been conducted to examine the relationship between large, complex societies and the presence of moralizing high gods. An association between monotheism and morality was first demonstrated by Swanson (1960). His comparison of fifty indigenous societies around the world demonstrated a positive relationship between political complexity and moral gods. Cross-cultural research conducted by Johnson extended Swanson's findings. "(A)s societies increased in political complexity gods were not necessarily more common or important, but they became more moralizing. As societies become larger and more structured, the types of gods people envisage become more involved with their moral conduct" (Johnson 2016:201–202). A significant and positive relationship has been demonstrated between the presence of such "big" moralizing gods "who tell people what they should and should not do" and measures of group size, social stratification, environmental resource levels, and levels of external conflict (Johnson 2016:201–202).

Experimental research indicates that these "big" moralizing gods who are at once omniscient, omnipotent, and omnipresent contribute to social cooperation by impacting individual choices and behaviors. Atkinson and colleagues note that "survey data and lab-based studies suggest that belief in (or priming the concept of) a powerful moralizing god can increase individual prosocial behavior . . . and point to the importance of the imagined presence of a supernatural monitor and the threat of punishment" (2015:266). Specific to this point is the finding by Shariff and Rhemtulla that "the more a nation's population believes in hell (on average), the lower the crime rates" (Johnson 2016:186). Social psychologist Ara Norenzayan (2013) maintains that big societies were not possible without big gods.

Wallace's religion "types" offer important insights into the variety, complexity, and adaptive functions of religious systems. His typology presents both costs and benefits of various religious systems and illustrates the flexibility of these systems in dynamically responding to changing collective action challenges. Among the greatest of such challenges are those of competition and conflict, both within and between social groups.

6 The Paradox of Violence and Religion

If the ultimate function of religion is to promote and enhance group solidarity, cooperation, and cohesion as argued by Durkhim (1954[1915]:62–63), Rappaport (1999:417), and others, then why is violence so ubiquitous across religious systems – both within social groups and between them?

Violence as a Proximate Mechanism of Religion

Evolutionary anthropologists view the ultimate function of religion to be its ability to create and promote cohesive, cooperative groups. Such groups enjoy competitive advantages over less cohesive groups in vigilance, reproductive opportunities, information sharing, and resource acquisition and defense. Cohesive, cooperative groups additionally experience reduced in-group reactive aggression and lower stress levels, thereby enhancing both the individual and inclusive fitness of group members. Humans gain additional advantages from social groups, including resource sharing, alloparenting, and technological advances; the benefits of large cohesive, cooperative groups are even greater. Yet, as previously noted, increases in the size of social groups and decreases in their genetic relatedness reduce the efficacy of inclusive fitness and reciprocity in deterring in-group aggression, deception, and free loading. Groups unable to resolve these problems face such collective action problems as overexploitation of resources, weakened defense systems, increased in-group aggression, and, most critically, increased potential for battlefield defection.

Historically and cross-culturally religion has comprised the preferred human institution for forging bonds of trust, inculcating social values, and creating cultural belief systems that foster group solidarity and promote cooperation. As discussed in Section 4, religious systems promote these outcomes through various proximate mechanisms, including powerful and socially omniscient supernatural agents, emotionally evocative and motivationally compelling sacred symbols, and metaphorical, memorable, and unfalsifiable beliefs. These religious symbols and beliefs attain their veracity and motivational force through association with emotionally powerful ritual experiences. Many ritual experiences evoke positive emotions that enhance affiliation and reduce stress. Ritual experiences that evoke strong negative emotions, however, are most memorable and motivationally powerful (Vaish et al. 2008). Darkened caves and cathedrals that arouse vigilance, malevolent masks and bleeding icons that evoke fear, and painful practices that elicit autonomic and somatic responses in ritual participants are common elements of religious systems. They infuse ritual experiences with emotional meaning that serve to sanctify the beliefs and symbols of religious systems, affording them veracity and imbuing them with motivational force. Threat, fear, and pain are costly, but they are also effective motivators of behavior. Violence, too, is a costly, but effective proximate mechanism of religion.

Across cultures and throughout history, violence has provided a useful tool for inculcating, authenticating, and corroborating religion. Religious violence – including sorcery, spirit possession, sacrifice, "sacred pain," and martyrdom – have been important elements in the mythology and ritual of religions throughout history. While healing shamans sought to propitiate the capricious and potentially evil spirits that reigned down illness and misfortune, "dark shamans" enlisted the assistance of such spirits in assault sorcery from North America to Africa to Australia (Wright 2015). Spirits of vindictive ancestors demanded homage and possessed the living. Bloodthirsty gods, hideous demons, and ghastly ghosts terrified and tormented humans across the religions of early Europe, Greece, and Rome (Alcorta and Sosis 2013). Aztec and Incan gods demanded that the still-beating hearts of victims be ripped from their chests in public ceremonies. Even contemporary religions require some sacrifice of adherents; many mandate self-inflicted violence through acts of penitence, deprivation, and self-mutilation. Fasting is common to all the world religions. Christian penance has historically included acts of self-mortification, including corporal punishment. During the annual Ashura festival, Shia Muslims commemorate the death of Muhammad's grandson Hussein through bloody rites of self-flagellation. Male circumcision is required in both Islam and Judaism. Religiously inspired terrorists and warriors inflict violence and terror on infidels, but they also inflict such violence on themselves. What is the purpose of such violence, and why is it so frequently a component of religion?

Religious Violence as a Costly Signal

Observers of religion have long noted the costliness of religious obligations (Sosis 2006:77–102). Even relatively simple, joyous rituals such as the *molimo* ceremony of the African Mbuti, where men and women dance and sing around a fire, entail time, energy, and resource costs. In contrast to such joyous rites, many sacred rituals subject participants to threatening, dangerous, and disgusting elements as well. The costliest rituals add to this violence, sacrifice, and pain.

Signaling theorists propose that costly religious practices and rituals have evolved in human groups as honest signals that advertise an individual's level of commitment to the goals and ideals of the group, both to oneself and to others (Sosis and Alcorta 2003:267). The ritualized mortification of the Taiwanese spirit medium described by Sutton (1990:99) exemplifies such signaling.

> Tiaotong, Tiaotong
> Barebodied, staggering as if insane,
> Goggle-eyed, hair disheveled,
> Raising a sword to cut his back.
> Slicing his tongue to write charms . . .
> Gritting his teeth to stand the pain,
> Dancing without pause.

By subjecting himself to intense pain through self-mutilation, the spirit medium sends a powerful signal to others regarding the honesty of his spirit possession. Anyone may claim to commune with invisible spirits, yet only those truly possessed would slice their own tongues and carve their own flesh. Shamans, ascetics, prophets, and martyrs who subject themselves to isolation, sleep deprivation, starvation, self-mortification, and torture provide similarly powerful signals of honesty and commitment that engender belief and adherence in others of their group.

Within shamanic religions, the highest costs are borne by the religious specialists themselves. These individuals voluntarily experience self-inflicted pain and violence. They undertake dangerous journeys to the spirit world to cure illness, avert or mitigate misfortune, and prevent disaster. Such journeys may require them to ingest nauseating and toxic substances, dance to exhaustion, self-mutilate, and enter dangerous trance states. Possession by the spirits with whom they communicate may result in injury, as well. The "dark shamans" who undertake the nefarious practice of assault sorcery also engage in painful and violent rituals with the potential to unleash terrible and uncontrollable consequences on the practitioners themselves (Wright 2015). The danger, pain, and violence experienced by the shaman send an incontrovertible message and reliable signal to others of the shaman's authenticity, as well as that of the spirits he/she seeks to appease.

Spirit possession is not confined to shamans nor to shamanic religions. It occurs across communal, Olympian, and monotheistic religious systems, as well. Possession rituals serve important political functions by safely conveying novel proposals and/or giving voice to the relatively powerless within social groups (Bubandt 2009:291). Since individuals possessed by spirits cannot be held responsible for the spirit's message, the authenticity of such possession is critical. The dangerous activities, violent behaviors, and self-injury that frequently occur during spirit possession serve as honest signals of possession, both authenticating the supernatural nature of the message relayed, and delimiting the culpability of the humans who relay it.

Social Control Theory of Violence

The violence of spirit possession affords a political mechanism for addressing inequalities and initiating social change within societies while safeguarding the relatively powerless. The violence of religious sacrifice in emergent stratified societies, however, communicates, consolidates, and consecrates the power of the rulers over the ruled.

Walter Burkert (2013) and Rene Girard (1977) have proposed ritualized sacrifice to be the genesis of religion. Eller has noted, however, that hunter-gatherer societies in which our species spent most of its existence are "the least likely to engage in sacrificial action" (2010:108). While religious violence, ritualized cannibalism, and death by sorcery are all features of numerous prestate societies (Wright 2015), "it is in highly formalized political systems – the Greco-Roman states, the Hawaiian and Dahomean kingdoms, and the Mayan and Aztec empires – that we find the most extensive and elaborated sacrificial traditions" (Eller 2010:108).

The "social control" theory of ritual sacrifice proposes that sacrificial ritual emerged to legitimize political authority in socially stratified societies and "promot(e) a shift to strictly inherited class systems" (Watts et al. 2016:228). According to this theory, public ceremonies of ritualized animal and human sacrifice by kings and priests initiated conscious and subconscious fear and threat responses in subjects that served to quell dissidence and ensure the compliance of those ruled. Empirical support for this thesis has recently been provided by Watts and colleagues (2016). They applied Bayesian phylogenetic methods to a sample of ninety-three geographically and culturally diverse traditional Austronesian cultures to test this theory. Their findings "strongly support the social control model and the contention that human sacrifice promoted and sustained the evolution of stratified societies" (Watts and colleagues 2016:228).

Adolescent Rites of Passage

The ritualized violence of shamanic journeys, spirit possession, and religious sacrifice constitutes a highly effective costly signal that authenticates the reality of religion's supernatural agents and communicates their power to intercede in human affairs. Nowhere is this power more evident, however, than in sacred adolescent rites of passage.

Nearly three-quarters of societies throughout the world conduct adolescent rites of passage. These rites vary widely from culture to culture. In some societies, such as the Yaghan of Patagonia and contemporary Judeo-Christian religions, adolescent rites of passage consist of little more than the oral transmission of knowledge. In other cultures, however, initiates may be subjected to kidnapping, forced seclusion, and numerous psychological and physical ordeals. Luiseño initiates were required to lie motionless while being bitten by angry hordes of ants. Tukuna girls had their hair plucked out. Nuer boys were scarified, and the Iatmul novice was incised with a small bamboo blade on his back. Baktaman initiation rituals were even more brutal and terrifying, with initiates being beaten and tortured (Barth 1975). In New Guinea, Ilahita Arapesh men dressed as frightening boars traditionally lacerated the penises of young boys with bamboo razors and pig incisors as part of initiation rites, and men publicly incised their own genitals after marriage (Tuzin 1976:337–339). In the traditional Mukanda ceremony of the African Ndembu, male elders dressed as masked ancestral spirits kidnapped and tortured young initiates. They concluded their lengthy rites with the circumcision of initiates by knife-wielding, red-stained elders – the "killers" of the boys – as participants watched (Turner 1969). The violence, pain, and terror of such rites are conveyed by Manny Twofeathers in his description of Native American Sun Dance Rites:

> I lay there on the ground, looking up into the sky. Then
> I handed Lessert my piercing bones. He got down on his
> knees next to me, and his father knelt by my left side. I felt
> both of them grab my chest and rub it with some dirt,

because I was sweaty and slippery. This way their thumbs
and fingers wouldn't slip. They pinched my skin, and I felt
as the knife went into my flesh. I felt a sharp, intense pain in
my chest, as if somebody had put a red-hot iron on my flesh.
I lost all sense of time. I couldn't hear any sounds. I didn't
feel the heat of the sun. I tried to grit my teeth, but
I couldn't . . . I prayed to the Creator to give me strength,
to give me courage . . . .When I stood up, I did feel pain.
I felt pain, but I also felt that closeness with the Creator . . .
The pain did not compare to what I was receiving from this
sacred experience . . . .I was tied to the tree with that rope as
securely as a child is tied to its mother by the umbilical cord.
The only way off that cord was by ripping myself off. Every
time I leaned back on my rope, I felt intense pain in my
chest. It became a raw ache that reached all the way down to
my toes . . . .It felt glorious and explosive. The energy was
high and brilliant . . . I went back, back. I looked at the tree
and said silently, "Grandfather, please give me strength."
I ran faster and faster and faster. I hit the end of the line.
I heard my flesh tear, rip, and pop. I saw the rope bouncing
way up in the tree. It dangled there for a second, then
dropped. While this was going on, I fell backwards. I had
broken loose . . . I was so happy, I let out a big yell.

(Glucklich 2001:147–148)

Sacred adolescent rites of passage are among the costliest of religious
rituals, with initiates subjected to beatings; isolation; food, water, and
sleep deprivation; consumption of toxic substances; tattooing, scarification,
genital mutilation, and a host of other psychological and physical ordeals.
They may result in physical disability, reproductive impairment, and even
death. Why do societies subject their adolescents to such violent rites, and
how do they impact the initiates involved?

The explicit function of adolescent rites of passage is to transform
children into socially responsible adults through the transmission of sacred
knowledge. This transformation is both social and psychological.

Adolescent rites of passage publicly communicate the transfer of statuses within a given social structure. Such rites clearly signal the status change of initiates and provide an institutionalized mechanism for affecting social and political change. Importantly, rites of passage transform ambiguous biological processes – at what point during puberty does a boy/girl become a man/woman? – into unambiguous digital information. Before the rite of passage initiates are boys and girls; they emerge from the rite as socially recognized men and women respectively with all the gender-related rights and requirements of adult status within their respective societies (Alcorta and Sosis 2020:4). These rites "help to establish a sense of social-emotional anchorage for the growing individual ... on the social map" (Cohen 1964:529). Rites of passage accomplish this by transmitting sociocultural knowledge to the initiate regarding adult roles and responsibilities, and by clearly communicating the transitioning of social statuses and identities within the social group. Rites of passage regenerate and transform social groups, as well. They provide a stabilizing mechanism for the smooth transfer of statuses within a given social structure, but they additionally afford an institutionalized mechanism for brokering power relations and creating social change within a society (Alcorta and Sosis 2020:4). Initiation rites change the status of individuals and may simultaneously alter the status of social groups within the larger collectivity. For societies organized along principles of descent, rites of passage have important political, as well as economic and reproductive consequences (Paige and Paige 1981).

In addition to their important impacts on the social and political relationships of a society, adolescent rites of passage alter initiates, as well. Numerous anthropologists have noted the transformative psychological effects of adolescent rites of passage (Alcorta 2021; Glucklich 2001; Turner 1969). The impacts of adolescent rites of passage on initiates can be profound. Even relatively benign rites of passage, such as those conducted in contemporary Christian and Buddhist training programs have short and long-term effects on autonomic, psychological, and behavioral measures (Alcorta 2016:110). In the United States, teen religious participation is positively associated with a broad array of prosocial behaviors, and significantly and negatively associated with cigarette smoking, alcohol and substance abuse, risky sexual behaviors, juvenile delinquency, and a host of psychological and physical disorders, including anxiety, depression, and suicidal behaviors (Alcorta 2016:110–111). Even comparatively mild exposure of adolescents to religious training can significantly impact their beliefs, behaviors, and biological indices. How does religion achieve these effects?

Brain changes that occur during adolescence make this developmental stage a particularly sensitive period for shaping a sense of self. Heightened activity in the emotion and reward processing regions of the adolescent brain and the dopaminergic "shift" in functional connectivity that occurs between executive, emotional, and reward processing regions optimize conditions for conditional and reinforcement learning (Wahlstrom et al. 2010). These changes provide a plastic neural substrate for learning social symbols and investing them with emotional meaning and motivational salience through processes of classical conditioning and reinforcement learning.

Religious rites of passage are optimally adapted for both emotionally charged conditioning and reward-based reinforcement learning (Alcorta and Sosis 2005:332–333). Sacred rites derive their power to inculcate socio-cultural values and influence individual behaviors from the strong emotions they evoke and the embodied experiences they create. Even relatively low-cost rites, such as participation in music-based communal rituals, serve to elicit feelings of joy and transcendence. Music, found in nearly all religions, engages the brain's reward system and stimulates the production of "feel good" neurochemicals such as dopamine, endorphins, and oxytocin (Chanda and Levitin 2013). Dopamine production underlies reinforcement learning (Daw 2007:1505). Oxytocin, a neuropeptide critical to interpersonal trust and affiliation (Ross and Young 2009:534), increases in-group favoritism and "to a lesser extent, out-group derogation" (De Dreu et al. 2011:1262). Additionally, oxytocin "can facilitate amygdala-dependent, socially reinforced learning and emotional empathy in men" (Hurlemann et al. 2010:4999). Participation in religious ritual elicits all these neurophysiological responses (Alcorta and Sosis 2013:577).

The ability of ritual to evoke both positive and negative affect is, of course, not specific to religion. Secular dances, concerts, and "raves" induce feelings of happiness and joy, and military boot camp elicits pain, shock, and awe. Such secular experiences have strong emotional impacts on participants also, particularly during adolescence. In contrast to secular ritual, however, religious ritual associates these embodied experiences and evoked emotions with abstract group symbols, including highly memorable counterintuitive beliefs and supernatural agents that prescribe and proscribe social behavior at a time in development when such agents and beliefs are most compelling and socially relevant. The metaphorical nature of these beliefs activates myriad subconscious social and emotional associations. The minimally counterintuitive beliefs of religious systems are easily remembered, difficult to forget, and almost impossible to "fake" by the uninitiated. These attributes render them powerful markers of group identity (Alcorta and Sosis 2005:328). Since they are unverifiable and unfalsifiable – that is, they cannot be proven or disproven – they endure (Rappaport 1999:281).

Rites of passage that couple emotionally rewarding experiences with fear-evoking pain and terror result in even more powerfully compelling embodied experiences, creating implicit and explicit memories. Such rites have pronounced psychological, physical, and neurophysiological impacts on initiates. Pain alters body states and, in doing so, alters our perceptions of time, space, and self (Damasio 1999:79). Glucklich has described "sacred pain" as "the mediating force that makes the acquisition of third-level (spiritual) reality possible" (2001:151), noting that "strong feelings induced by pain affect our capacity to perceive and know reality" (2001:150). Anthropologist T. O. Beidelman describes the pain in traditional East African Kaguru initiation ceremonies as "so incontestably real that it seems to confer its quality of 'incontestable reality' on that power that has brought it into being" (1997:179).

Violent experiences during adolescence have profound effects on subsequent aggressive behavior, as well (see Section 2). Developmental changes occurring during adolescence in neurotransmitter systems and brain structures critical for emotional, motivational, and social/moral functions maximize opportunities for personal experiences to impact both epigenetic and learning processes. The psychologically and physically demanding ordeals of violent adolescent rites of passage, like exposure to abuse, conflict and warfare, prime the threat response systems of initiates and produce higher levels of aggressive response (see Section 2). Concomitantly, the association of abstract group symbols with the extreme emotions and powerful autonomic responses elicited by painfully violent ritual experiences can invest these abstractions with strong motivational significance through processes of classical conditioning and reinforcement learning (Alcorta and Sosis 2013:581).

Violent ritual practices frequently alter the physical appearance of initiates. Ritual practices of tattooing, scarification, tooth ablation, and circumcision etch indelible neurophysiological alterations in the brains of initiates as well as permanent markers of group membership on their bodies. These signals powerfully influence social interactions both within and between groups. Rappaport elegantly describes the impacts of such markers on the initiates themselves:

> When that sign is carved on the body the abstract is not only made substantial but immediate ... and if the mark is indelible, as in the case of the subincision, the excised canine, the lopped finger, the scarified face, chest, or back, it is ever-present. As the abstract is made alive and concrete by the living substance of men and women, so are men and women predicated by the abstractions which they themselves realize (1999:149).

Violent initiation rites sanctify group values and invest group symbols and beliefs with strong motivational force. Extreme rituals are highly effective in promoting prosociality (Xygalatas et al. 2013:1605). Groups of initiates who jointly experience such rites bond as "brothers in arms" prepared to give their lives for one another and for the sacred beliefs that bind them.

Adolescent Rites of Passage and Social Complexity

Nearly 70 percent of traditional societies studied by anthropologists conduct adolescent religious rites of passage (Lutkehaus & Roscoe 1995:xiv). Most entail relatively simple rituals involving single adolescent females at first menarche. Such female rites are recorded for 50–60 percent of traditional societies, while individual male rites of passage are found in only 30–40 percent of traditional cultures. In contrast, rites of passage involving groups of age-graded cohorts more frequently involve males. Approximately 30 percent of societies throughout the world conduct male group initiation rites, as compared to only 10 percent that conduct group rites for females (Alcorta and Sosis 2020:5).

The presence or absence of adolescent rites of passage in a society, as well as the particular forms these rites take, significantly correlate with social complexity in a U-shaped pattern. Research by Schlegel and colleagues found that "initiation ceremonies follow an evolutionary track. Ceremonies for girls are predominant in simple societies; ceremonies for boys become equally frequent at the middle range; in complex societies, these ceremonies tend to be absent" (Schlegel and Barry 1980:710).

The wide variance in the occurrence, form, and costliness of adolescent rites of passage was examined by Sosis and colleagues in a cross-cultural study utilizing data collected from the Human Relations Area Files electronic databases (eHRAF). Findings revealed that prestate societies with the most violent adolescent rites of passage, as measured by psychological and physical ordeals, were also those most frequently engaging in warfare. High-risk conditions of inter-tribal warfare render individual incentive to defect and free ride particularly great. These researchers concluded that "costly male rites signal commitment and promote solidarity among males who must organize for warfare" (Sosis et al. 2007:234). Wrangham asserts that "When self-sacrificial war practices are found in humans . . . they result from cultural systems of reward, punishment, and coercion rather than evolved adaptations to greater risk-taking" (2012:5). The violent and costly adolescent rites of passage that occur across societies frequently engaging in warfare represent just such a system, with its indelible imprints of ritualized joy, pain, and violence on both the minds and bodies of initiates.

Religious Violence and Modern Monotheism

Like the young initiates of sacred rites of passage, most contemporary religiously inspired terrorists begin their militant life during adolescence. Victoroff observes that the "typical development of terrorist sympathies perhaps follows an arc: young adolescents are plastic in their political orientation and open to indoctrination. Positions harden later in adolescence . . . [and] many retired 'terrorists' reveal a mellowing of attitude" (2005:28). By the time those raised in a culture of martyrdom reach adolescence they are already prepared to sacrifice themselves without further indoctrination. Images of flag-waving jihadis rolling across vast swaths of desert have become dominant themes in the public media of the early twenty-first century. These images are menacing, as they are meant to be. Yet, beneath many of the black balaclava that shroud the heads of these terrorists are the smooth countenances of young boys and the barely stubbled faces of teens. Many young recruits are the orphaned children of those killed by terrorists. Traumatized by the slaying of their families, these youth face a stark choice between conversion to the terrorist cause or death. Some recruits are simply kidnapped; others are "sold" by impoverished and destitute families; still others voluntarily join the terrorists as local economies are shattered, secular schools are shuttered, and villages and their resources are seized (Alcorta 2021:99–100).

Once recruited, these youth are taken to camps where they undergo indoctrination. Reports from those who have escaped paint a grim picture. Recruits are first desensitized by watching videos of beheadings. The humiliation, torture, and beheading of captured combatants follow. Severed heads are passed around the group to further dehumanize the enemy, and decapitated bodies are publicly displayed. The young recruits are encouraged to revile and defile them. Boys learn decapitation techniques. Those who resist are tortured; those who try to escape are shot. The program is brutal and barbaric; it is also effective in desensitizing recruits, dehumanizing the enemy, and indoctrinating and training young terrorists able and willing to kill, even if such killing requires them to sacrifice their own lives (Alcorta 2021:99–100). Terrorist training camps effectively employ fear, violence, and pain in rituals reminiscent of costly adolescent rites of passage (Nesser 2008:234–256).

Psychologist Brian Barber, who studies youth experiences with violence and war, explains that personal experiences with violence shape how youths respond to the conflict in which they are raised. According to Barber, "much of identity can be sourced externally, in that political conflict can literally divide and define who one is (ethnically, religiously, politically, culturally, etc.)" (2008:306). The impacts of violence on youth identity have been well established. Ongoing exposure to violence is significantly and positively correlated with greater anxiety and more aggressive behaviors (see Section 2). Like violent and costly adolescent rites of passage, the brutality and violence of religiously inspired terrorist training camps provide highly effective "cultural systems of rewards, punishment, and coercion" (Wrangham and Glowacki 2012:5) that serve to overcome individual self-interest and promulgate self-sacrifice on behalf of a community bound through sacred beliefs.

Violence as an Ultimate Cause

On January 7, 2015, two brothers armed with assault rifles forced their way into the Parisian offices of the satirical French newspaper, *Charlie Hebdo*. Once inside, they brutally gunned down eleven employees before fleeing the scene and taking the life of a twelfth victim. These slayings were initiated in response to the publication of cartoons depicting the Prophet Mohammed. Five years later a lone attacker assaulted a middle school teacher on the streets of a Parisian suburb, killing and beheading him in cold blood – again, in retaliation for such cartoons. The *Charlie Hebdo* murders shocked and confounded many Western observers. Yet, they represent but one manifestation of a much deeper, and broader relationship between religion and proactive violence that is likely to be as old as religion itself. Just as violence constitutes a very effective proximate mechanism of religion; religion serves as an excellent proximate mechanism for violence, as well (Kiper and Sosis 2021).

Framing the Conflict

Religiously inspired terrorism is but one example of how religion may be used to effectively promote violence. Yet, the attributes that render religion a particularly effective tool of violence for terrorists are the same attributes that render it an effective tool for conducting religious Crusades and justifying wars of divine kingdoms and religious nation-states, as well. Deconstructing religiously inspired terrorism is relevant for understanding how religion, in general, facilitates proactive violence.

Numerous researchers have argued that terrorists have political, not religious goals (Bloom 2005; Juergensmeyer 2003; Pape 2005). Juergensmeyer (2003) maintains that while religion is not the root cause of most conflicts involving terror, religion is the means by which terrorists translate a local political struggle into a cosmic war. By transforming a political struggle into a divine mission, kings, emperors and terrorists confer moral legitimacy on their actions, while eternal rewards render those actions worthy of self-sacrifice (Sosis et al. 2012:238). In other words, terrorists often frame their disputes in religious rather than political terms. This has various advantages, most significantly in motivating others to sacrifice themselves for the cause. This transformation from political to religious struggle encourages actors to perceive that they are participating in something of divine significance that transcends individual self-interest (Sosis et al. 2012:238). Religious scholar Margo Kitts has argued that for the suicide bombers of 9/11 participation in the religious rituals enacted during their last night together served to "heighten the communicational register and bind the actors to a dense metaphorical domain" in which they viewed themselves as religious warriors and perceived their pending suicide to be a holy sacrifice (2010:283). Among Sikh militants in the Punjab, Juergensmeyer describes joining the struggle as "motivated by the heady sense of spiritual fulfillment and the passion of holy war" (2004a:2).

Some contemporary terrorists have been highly adept in shaping world views so that they are consistent with their own views. Bin Laden, for instance, was particularly successful in transforming his local grievance (getting US troops off "Muslim" soil) into a cosmic clash between civilizations. The use of religion to transform local power struggles into cosmic conflicts benefits terrorist groups who may otherwise be viewed as economically and politically self-serving. In an age of instantaneous electronic communications, such religious framing of essentially local conflicts serves to broaden both the ideological and geographic base of terrorism. It also serves to extend the horizon for victory. Terrorists perceive that they are fighting a cosmic war in divine time, thus eliminating incentives to "win" within one's own lifetime (Sosis et al. 2012:238–239). Commenting on an interview with Hamas leader Abdul Aziz Rantisi, Juergensmeyer observes that "[i]n his calculation, the struggles of God can endure for eons" (2004b:35).

Moral Justification

Religion facilitates terrorists' goals by providing moral legitimacy to their cause, as well (Juergensmeyer 2003). Religion is highly effective in creating motivationally powerful values, as illustrated by the Charlie Hebdo murders. Atran notes that "the willingness to fight and die among frontline combatants in Iraq from 2015 to 2016 was greatest for those who fought for sacred values" (2021:1063). Adherence to sacred values leads to perceived moral obligations. One is obliged to act 'independently of the likelihood of success' . . . because believers could not live with themselves if they did not" (Atran 2006:138). All contemporary world religions impose a moral framework upon their adherents, thereby enabling terrorists to present their conflicts in morally absolute dichotomies, such as good versus bad or righteous versus evil. While legitimizing ones' own cause, religions are particularly effective at demonizing those with opposing views. The history of religion is replete with examples in which in-group passions are aroused and out-group hatreds are dangerously ignited. Indeed, one consistent predictor of suicide terrorism is a religious difference between the perpetrator and victim (Pape 2005). This occurs even when the terrorist group appears to have secular motivations, such as the LTTE, who are Hindus fighting a Buddhist majority. In Berman and Laitin's (2005) extensive sample of suicide terrorism, almost 90 percent of the attacks were aimed at victims of a different religion (Sosis et al. 2012:238–239).

Spiritual and Eternal Rewards

Religion not only provides a divine dimension and moral legitimacy to proactive violence; it also defines the rewards that combatants can attain. After considering the benefits that Sikh militants attain, Juergensmeyer concluded that "[t]he reward for these young men was the religious experience in the struggle itself: the sense that they were participating in something greater than themselves" (2004a:2). In addition to such spiritual rewards of transcendence, religion may also explicitly offer benefits in the afterlife that can rarely be matched in this world. The 9/11 hijackers all believed that they "would meet in the highest heaven" (Lincoln 2003:98), which we can assume helped them rationalize their actions (Sosis et al. 2012:239).

Religious Symbols, Myths, and Rituals

As we have discussed herein and elsewhere (Sosis and Alcorta 2008), religious beliefs and values are effective mechanisms for facilitating proactive violence and advancing terrorist goals. Religion's most significant role in terrorism and proactive violence, however, may be its incorporation of emotionally evocative and highly memorable symbols, myths, and rituals that serve to individually motivate and collectively unify diverse individuals under a common banner. All terrorist groups face the challenge of creating group commitment and individual devotion to a common cause. Anthropologists have long noted that fundamental "faith-based" elements of religion, that is symbols, myths, and rituals, foster this in-group commitment better than any other social institution. Not surprisingly, secular and religious terrorists alike maintain communal rituals and initiation rites that communicate an individual's level of commitment to the group (Atran 2003). For religious combatants, cohesiveness is further fostered through emotionally powerful and motivationally salient religious symbols, which "often become focal points in occupations involving a religious difference" (Pape 2005:89). And of course, martyrdom itself means to sacrifice one's life for one's faith. Religion provides the rituals and symbols to both motivate and memorialize these local heroes, thereby affording them an otherwise unattainable status that is also eternal (Sosis et al. 2012:240). Pape observes that "[s]uicide terrorist organizations commonly cultivate 'sacrificial myths' that include elaborate sets of symbols and rituals to mark an individual attacker's death as a contribution to the nation" (2005:29).

The elements of religious ritual that render it a powerful mechanism for creating highly cohesive, cooperative, and committed social groups are most adaptive in warfare. The ability of religion to create and clearly delineate in- and out-groups, to imbue group beliefs and values with the compelling motivational force of sacred truths, and to subordinate individual self-interest to that of the larger social group are highly effective tools for promulgating proactive intergroup violence. The use of religion to convert a political conflict into a moral one illustrates what Strathern and Stewart (2005) have termed "the role of the imaginary" in religious violence. When that imaginary encompasses unfalsifiable, socially omniscient and powerful gods, the mandates are unequivocal and judgments are eternal.

7 Religion and Human Evolution

Exactly when religion emerged in human evolution is impossible to know. Early human populations, like those of our closest primate kin, no doubt engaged in ritual to communicate social information and control reactive aggression within the group. Group sizes of these early modern humans, like those of our Neanderthal cousins, were likely small.

To date, the earliest suggestion of symbolic behavior in early modern human groups occurs at the 320,000-year-old site of Olorgesailie, Kenya. Here, gouges in black and red rocks and minerals have been interpreted by some as the product of pigment creation associated with ritualized behaviors (Brooks et al. 2018:90). Possible evidence of trade networks at Olorgesailie has been suggested, as well. If so, rudimentary human symbolic ritual may have emerged to create intergroup alliances, as proposed by archaeologist Brian Hayden (1987). Ritualized ochre markings may have initially served to define and identify members of trade networks. In the absence of more definitive evidence, however, the evidence remains controversial and the interpretations speculative.

Widely accepted evidence of symbolic behavior does not appear in the archaeological record until some 200,000 years later. Ground red ochre and worked red ochre lumps incised with abstract etchings dated between 130,000–70,000 years ago have been found at various sites throughout South Africa (Marean 2010:58–59). Based on ethnographic analogies, archaeologists have concluded that these artifacts are evidence of symbolic ritual in the early modern human populations inhabiting these sites. At the 110,000-year-old South African site of Pinnacle Point, red ochre lumps are found in association with highly sophisticated technologies, including advanced microlith and projectile technologies, poisons, and hot rock technology (Marean 2010:58–59). Ochre lumps found at the Blombos Cave site bear abstract etchings incised some 70,000 years ago (Henshilwood et al. 2001:668).

These coastal sites were inhabited by large, sedentary populations at a time when many hominin populations throughout Africa were migrating and dying out due to changing climatic conditions. These South African populations developed new technologies to successfully exploit novel resources, including mussels and other marine life, as well as hard-to-find and difficult-to-extract tubers (Marean 2010:54–61).

Large population sizes afforded these groups numerous advantages including a broader, deeper gene pool for dampening demographic fluctuations (Hammel 2005:2251–2252) and avoiding genetic bottlenecks

(Marean 2010:55). Larger groups included more juveniles and adolescents. Across societies, it is primarily juveniles who try out novel resources and behaviors as they engage in "play" (Diamond 1997:118). New resources and innovative approaches would have been particularly important for populations adapting to variable and shifting ecologies. A larger cohort of adolescents would have provided explorers and warriors at a time of extensive migration and intergroup competition, while additional elders represented a deeper, broader knowledge base. Across traditional human societies, elders provide critical information regarding the location of long-term cyclical resources, such as waterholes, that contribute to group survival. Elders also serve as caretakers, cooks, and alloparents, thereby reducing maternal investment and freeing mothers for resource acquisition. The consequent shortening of interbirth intervals would have increased reproductive rates in these populations. All such demographically driven benefits of larger population sizes would have been particularly important in the erratically changing environmental conditions of the African Middle Stone Age.

Yet, large social groups also introduce new problems of competition, freeloading, and possible defection (Krebs and Dawkins 1984:120–133), problems which escalate with increasing group size and decreasing genetic relatedness (Alcorta and Sosis 2013:586). Fluctuating environmental conditions during this period would have contributed to intense selection pressures for all early hominin populations. Escalating levels of stress-driven reactive aggression within social groups, as well as greater competition and proactive aggression between them, is likely to have occurred. Increases in brain size in both Neanderthal and early modern human populations during this period no doubt reflect intense selection for social and technological adaptations that afforded these populations competitive advantages. By 300,000 years ago brain size in both *Homo sapiens* and *H. neanderthalensis* "fell within the range of present-day humans" (Neubauer et al. 2018). Neanderthal brains grew larger while brain development continued to follow the predominantly precocial developmental pattern of other hominids. The increases in brain sizes of modern human populations, however, were accompanied by a change in the developmental trajectory, as well. In these populations brain development shifted from a predominantly prenatal to extended postnatal development pattern. Physical anthropologist Phillip Gunz and his colleagues note, "Neandertals and modern humans reach comparable adult brain sizes via different developmental pathways. The differences between these two human groups are most prominent directly after birth, a critical phase for cognitive development" (Gunz et al. 2012:300).

This change in early modern human brain development patterns to more altricial neonates with less fully developed brains has traditionally been explained as an adaptation to ensure that the head of large-brained newborns could fit through a bipedally narrowed birth canal. Yet, the fossil evidence suggests that the bipedal Neanderthals successfully birthed precocial, large-brained neonates (Gunz et al. 2012:300). Moreover, altriciality is a life history adaptation found across numerous species, including large social carnivores. This life history pattern can provide advantages for species inhabiting widely fluctuating environments and/or those exploiting rapidly changing resources. The birthing of altricial young shifts maternal investment from predominantly prenatal to postnatal development thereby reducing maternal investment when resources are insufficient for successful nurturance of offspring. When environmental conditions are good and resources available, mothers can successfully rear less developed offspring. More altricial neonates allow mothers to optimize their maternal investment under conditions of environmental uncertainty. For species that engage in alloparenting, altriciality may increase reproductive rates, as well, since mothers can shorten interbirth intervals by offloading investment costs through shared caretaking of young. These advantages of altriciality would have been particularly relevant for early modern human groups given the high energetic costs of large brains and the increased reproductive rates made possible by alloparenting and the cooking and sharing of resources.

Altriciality introduces a second important benefit in fluctuating environments, as well. The birthing of neonates with incompletely developed brains creates an opportunity for environmental experiences to impact brain development through epigenetic and learning processes. The ability to "shape" more adaptive behaviors within specific environments on shorter time scales allows for greater behavioral flexibility and innovation.

Colonizing species continuously entering new environments, and social carnivores faced with the need to jointly innovate hunting strategies within dynamically changing ecologies can both benefit from the brain plasticity afforded by the extended postnatal brain development of altriciality.

8 Conclusion

Early modern humans were both colonizers and social hunters. Whether the shift in brain development patterns in early modern humans was initially a solution to an obstetrical dilemma, or a primary life history adaptation, it altered the course of human evolution. By creating "an opportunity for experience to influence neural development" (Johnson 2001:475), altriciality and its associated extended human brain plasticity provided a fertile field for sowing the seeds of human symbolic communication, extended social cooperation, and human culture.

Throughout human evolution, religion, aggression, and violence have played important roles in sowing those seeds. The sacred symbols of religion have provided humans the means of creating large, cooperative social groups, subordinating individual self-interest to that of the social group, decreasing in-group stress, and reducing reactive aggression. Aggression, violence, and the threat of violence have, in turn, served as powerful proximate mechanisms for achieving these ends.

Ironically, selection for religion and the larger cooperative social groups it enables has likely been driven by ongoing competition between groups and the proactive aggression it has spawned. Religion's ability to: (1) create and cohesify large cooperative groups; (2) imbue unfalsifiable supernatural agents, sacred beliefs, and socially significant symbols with emotional salience and motivational force; (3) subordinate individual interests to those of the social group; and (4) sanctify moral systems that justify proactive violence and aggression against the "Other" render it a powerful force and an effective adaptation.

Religious systems, like other complex adaptations, vary widely in their constituent components, benefits, and costs. Moreover, religious systems, like other evolved traits, are only adaptive in relation to specific ecologies. The thousands of religious communities that have not withstood the test of time point to adaptive constraints and illustrate how religious systems can become inflexible and unresponsive to changing socioecological needs. Yet, religion's recurrence and endurance throughout history is testament to its extraordinary adaptability across diverse socioecologies.

Not only do functioning religious systems adapt to local socioecological conditions, but adherents generally fail to recognize religious change. Rather, adherents experience partaking in an eternally consistent and changeless tradition. Anthropologist Roy Rappaport (1999) argues that religions achieve this sleight of hand through a hierarchy of religious discourse. He claims there is an inverse relationship between the material specificity of a religious claim and the durability of the claim. Religious ideas are hierarchically organized within communities and at the apex of a community's conceptual hierarchy is what Rappaport refers to as ultimate sacred postulates, such as the Shahada, Shema, or Vandana Ti-sarana for Muslim, Jewish, and Buddhist communities respectively. Rappaport describes ultimate sacred postulates as unfalsifiable and unverifiable because they lack material specificity. They are highly resistant to change yet, because of their ambiguity, they may be reinterpreted anew each generation. Below ultimate sacred postulates in the religious hierarchy are various cosmological axioms, ritual proscriptions, commandments, directives, social rules and other religious assertions that do experience varying levels of change, depending on their material specificity.

Religious rules adjust and transform all the time but such changes are understood by those who experience them as an intensification of acceptance. Religions rarely invalidate the old completely; change occurs by adding to previous practices and beliefs and elaborating upon them, while other beliefs and practices slip away unnoticed. Once sacralization is internalized, it is indeed very difficult to convince adherents that something consecrated is no longer holy. Hence, when undergoing change, religions often retain the most sacralized elements and augment them. Missionaries often retain the dates of pagan celebrations, for example, and Jewish prayers appear in the Catholic Mass.

Rappaport's hierarchy of religious discourse helps explain why religious extremism – which often results in violence – is so dangerous. Extremism occurs when low-level directives and social rules are attributed the sanctity – that is, the unquestionableness – of ultimate sacred postulates. When social rules such as those that deny women the opportunity to drive, divorce, or delve sacred texts, or claims such as "the sun revolves around the earth" become highly sanctified it impedes the ability of religious systems to adapt to new social, political, ecological, and economic conditions. Religious systems that lose their adaptability become dangerous to the societies in which they exist, and to themselves, because they absolutize the relative. Under extremist regimes, for example, social rules about attire, food consumption, gender roles, and violence can become more sanctified than life itself. In other words, extremism can turn the hierarchy of religious discourse upside down. Rappaport suggests that religions that oversanctify social rules are unsustainable. To survive, religions must adapt and religious extremism impedes adaptive flexibility. We currently have little understanding of how long extremist groups can endure despite their tendency to ossify social rules. Tragically, even if such groups are ephemeral, many of them seem intent on destroying others as they destroy themselves.

Throughout human evolution, successful religious systems have provided a mechanism for resolving collective action problems by engendering social cooperation, reducing in-group reactive aggression, and optimizing out-group proactive aggression. Secular contemporary nation-states achieve these objectives through powerful political systems capable of controlling in-group aggression with domestic police and monopolizing proactive, out-group aggression through military might. Like prestate traditional societies, these powerful and well-established polities also face ongoing problems of internal dissension, fragmentation, and insurrection. Many such entities co-opt various proximate mechanisms of religion, such as emotionally evocative symbols and music-based communal ritual, to address such dissension and promulgate cooperation.

History suggests, however, that the unverifiable and unfalsifiable ultimate sacred postulates of religion, including socially omniscient supernatural agents and sanctified moral truths, are foundational in establishing and maintaining the human trust and cooperation required for large and long-lasting social groups. Rappaport maintained that "human organization could not have come into existence, or persisted, in the absence of ultimate sacred propositions and the sanctification of discourse" (1971:29). It is, therefore, not surprising that religion remains an important element in individual lives and human societies throughout the world. And as we have shown throughout this volume, religion's adaptive value lies in its ability to unite individuals for extraordinary feats of cooperation, as well as astonishing acts of violence.

References

Adachi, Paul J. C. and Teena Willoughby. "The Effect of Violent Video Games on Aggression: Is It More Than Just the Violence?" *Aggression and Violent Behavior* 16/1 (2011):55–62. http://doi.org/10.1016/j.avb.2010.12.002

Alcorta, Candace. "Religion, Social Signaling and Health: A Psychoneuroimmunological Approach." *Religion, Brain, and Behavior* 7/3 (2016):1–3. http://doi.org/10.1080/2153599X.2016.1156559

Alcorta, Candace. "Cerebral Lateralization and Religion: The Roles of Ritual and the DMN." *Religion, Brain, and Behavior* 9/4 (2019):339–345. https://doi.org/10.1080/2153599X.2019.1604412

Alcorta, Candace. "Adolescence and Religion: An Evolutionary Perspective." In *The Oxford Handbook of Evolutionary Psychology and Religion*, eds. James R. Liddle and Todd K. Shackelford. New York: Oxford University Press, 2021. 99–116.

Alcorta, Candace and Richard Sosis. "Ritual, Emotion, and Sacred Symbols: The Evolution of Religion as an Adaptive Complex." *Human Nature* 16/4 (December 2005):323–359. http://doi.org/10.1007/s12110-005-1014-3

Alcorta, Candace S. and Richard Sosis. "Ritual, Religion, and Violence: An Evolutionary Perspective." In *The Oxford Handbook of Religion and Violence*, eds. Mark Juergensmeyer, Margo Kitts, and Michael Jerryson. Oxford: Oxford University Press, 2013. 517–596.

Alcorta, Candace S. and Richard Sosis. "Adolescent Religious Rites of Passage: An Anthropological Perspective." In *The Encyclopedia of Child and Adolescent Development*, eds. Stephen Hupp and Jeremy D. Jewell. New York: Wiley & Sons, 2020. 1–12.

American Psychological Association. *APA Resolution on Violent Video Games. February 2020 Revision to the 2015 Resolution*, 2020. apa.org/about/policy/resolution-violent-video-games.pdf

Arendt, Hannah. *On Violence*. New York: Harcourt, 1970.

Atkinson, Q. D., A. J. Latham, and J. Watts. "Are Big Gods a Big Deal in the Emergence of Big Groups?" *Religion, Brain, and Behavior* 5/4 (2015):266–342.

Atran, Scott. *In Gods We Trust: The Evolutionary Landscape of Religion*. Oxford: Oxford University Press, 2002.

Atran, Scott. "Genesis of Suicide Terrorism." *Science* 299/5612 (March 7, 2003):1534–1539.doi: 10.1126/science.1078854

Atran, Scott. "Mishandling Suicide Terrorism." *Washington Quarterly* 27 (2004):67–90.

Atran, Scott. "The Moral Logic and Growth of Suicide Terrorism." *Washington Quarterly* 29 (2006):127–147.

Atran, Scott. "Psychology of Transnational Terrorism and Extreme Political Conflict." *Annual Review of Psychology* 14/6 (2021): 471–501. http://doi.org/10.1146/annurev-ppsych-010419–050800

Atran, Scott and Ara Norenzayan. "Religion's Evolutionary Landscape: Counterintuition, Commitment, Compassion, Communion." *Behavioral and Brain Sciences* 27/6 (December 2004):730–770. http://doi.org/10 .1017/s0140525x04000172

Austin, J. *Zen and the Brain*. Cambridge, MA: MIT Press, 1998.

Barber, Brian. "Contrasting Portraits of War: Youths Varied Experiences with Political Violence in Bosnia and Palestine." *International Journal of Behavioral Development* 32 (2008):298–309.

Barnow, Sven and Harald-J. Freyberger. "The Family Environment in Early Life and Aggressive Behavior in Adolescents and Young Adults." *Neurobiology of Aggression*, ed. Mark P. Mattson. New Jersey: Humana Press, 2003. 213–230.

Barth, Fredrick. *Ritual and Knowledge Among the Baktaman of New Guinea*. New Haven, CT: Yale University Press, 1975.

Basso, Ellen. *The Kalapalo Indians of Central Brazil*. Long Grove, IL: Waveland Press, 1988.

Becker, Judith. "Anthropological Perspectives on Music and Emotion." In *Music and Emotion*, eds. P. Juslin and J. Sloboda. Oxford: Oxford University Press, 2001. 135–160.

Beidelman, T. O. *The Cool Knife: Imagery of Gender, Sexuality, and Moral Education in Kaguru Initiation Ritual*. Washington, DC: Smithsonian Institution Press, 1997.

Bellah, Robert. *Religion in Human Evolution*. Cambridge, MA: Belknap Press, 2011.

Bering, J. M. "The Evolutionary History of an Illusion: Religious Causal Beliefs in Children and Adults." In *Origins of the Social Mind: Evolutionary Psychology and Child Development*, eds. Bruce J. Ellis and David F. Bjorklund. New York: Guilford Press, 2005. 411–437.

Bering, Jesse M. and David F. Bjorklund. "The Natural Emergence of Reasoning About the Afterlife as a Developmental Regularity." *Developmental Psychology* 40/2 (2004):217–233. http://doi.org/10.1037/0012–1649.40.2.217

Berman, E. and D. Laitin. "Hard Targets: Theory and Evidence on Suicide Attacks." *NBER Working Paper 11740*. Cambridge, MA: National Bureau of Economic Research, 2005.

Berman, E. and D. Laitin. "Religion, Terrorism and Public Goods: Testing the Club Model." *Journal of Public Economics* 92 (2008):1942–1967.

Blair, R., R. James, and Dennis S. Charney. "Emotion Regulation: An Affective Neuroscience Approach." In *Neurobiology of Aggression*, ed. Mark P. Mattson. Totowa, NJ: Humana Press, 2003. 21–32.

Bloch, Maurice. *Ritual, History, and Power*. London: The Athlone Press, 1989.

Bloom, M. *Dying to Kill: The Global Phenomenon of Suicide Terror*. New York: Columbia University Press, 2005.

Brooks, Alison, J. E. Yellen, R. Potts, et al. "Long Distance Stone Transport and Pigment Use in the Earliest Middle Stone Age." *Science* 360/6384 (April 2018):90–94. http://doi.org/10.1126/SCIENCE AAO2646

Bubandt, Nils. "Interview with an Ancestor: Spirits as Informants and the Politics of Possession in North Maluku." *Ethnography* 10/3 (2009): 291–316. http://doi.org/10.1177/1466138109339044

Bulbulia, Joseph and Richard Sosis. "Signaling Theory and the Evolution of Religious Cooperation." *Religion* 41 (2011):363–388.

Burkert, Walter. "Sacrificial Violence: A Problem in Ancient Religions." In *Oxford Handbook of Religion and Violence*, eds. Mark Juergensmeyer, Margo Kitts, and Michael Jerryson. New York: Oxford University Press, 2013. 437–453.

Bushman, Brad J. "Editorial Overview: Aggression and Violence." *Current Opinion in Psychology* 19 (2018): iv–vi.

Carhart-Harris, R. L. and K. J. Friston. "The Default-Mode, Ego-Functions and Free-Energy: A Neurobiological Account of Freudian Ideas." *Brain* 133/4 (April 2010): 1265–1283. http://doi.org/10.1093/brain/awq010

Carter, C. S. "Neuroendocrine Perspectives on Social Attachment and Love." *Psychoneuroendocrinology* 23/8 (1998):779–818. http://doi.org/10.1016/s0306-4530(98)00055-9. PMID: 9924738.

Chanda, M. L. and D. J. Levitin. "The Neurochemistry of Music." *Trends in Cognitive Sciences* 17/4 (2013):179–193.

Chaves, Mark, Mary Ellen Konieczny, Kraig Beyerlein, and Emily Barman. "National Congregations Study: Background, Methods, and Selected Results." *Journal for the Scientific Study of Religion* 38/4 (1999):458–476. http://doi.org/10.2307/1387606

Clayton, Martin, Kelly Kalubowski, Tuomas Eerola, et al. "Interpersonal Entrainment in Music Performance: Theory, Method, and Model." *Music Perception* 38/2 (2020):136–194. http://doi.org/10.1525/mp.2020.38.2.136

Coccaro, E., J. Fanning, K. Phan, and R. Lee. "Serotonin and Impulsive Aggression." *CNS Spectrums* 20/3 (2015):295–302. http://doi.org/10.1017/S109285291500031

Cohen, Y. A. "The Establishment of Identity in a Social Nexus: The Special Case of Initiation Ceremonies and Their Relation to Value and Legal Systems." *American Anthropologist* 66 (1964):529–552.

Corrigan, John, ed. "Introduction: Emotions Research and the Academic Study of Religion." In *Religion and Emotion: Approaches and Interpretations*. Oxford: Oxford University Press, 2004. 3–32.

Crawford, Neta C. and Catherine Lutz. "Human Cost of Post-9/11 Wars: Direct War Deaths in Major War Zones." In *Twenty Years of War. Costs of War Project*, eds. Neta C. Crawford and C. Lutz. Watson Institute, Brown University, 2019:1–5.

Dahl, R. E. "Adolescent Brain Development: A Period of Vulnerabilities and Opportunities." *Adolescent Brain Development: Vulnerabilities and Opportunities. Keynote Address. Annals of the New York Academy of Sciences* 1021/1 (June 2004). http://doi.org/10.1196/annals.1308.001

Damasio, Antonio. *Descartes' Error: Emotion, Reason, and the Human Brain.* New York: Avon Books, 1994.

Damasio, Antonio. *The Feeling of What Happens: Body and Emotion in the Making of Consciousness*. Boston, MA: Mariner Books, 1999.

Davis, Arran, J. Taylor, and E. Cohen. "Social Bonds and Exercise: Evidence for a Reciprocal Relationship." *PloS one* 10/8 (Aug. 2015) e0136705. http://doi.org/10.1371/journal.pone.0136705

Daw, N. D. "Dopamine: At the Intersection of Reward and Action." *Nature Neuroscience* 10 (2007):1505–1507.

Dawson, Joe and Scott Sleek. "The Fluidity of Time: Scientists Uncover How Emotions Alter Time Perception." *Observer*, Association for Psychological Science 31/8 (September 28, 2018):24–27.

De Boer, Sietse F. "Animal Models of Excessive Aggression: Implications for Human Aggression and Violence." *Current Opinion in Psychology* 19 (2018):81–87.

De Dreu, Carsten, L. L. Greer, G. A. Van Kleef, S. Shalvi, and M. J. Handgraaf. "Oxytocin Promotes Human Ethnocentrism." *Proceedings of the National Academy of Sciences of the United States of America* 108/4 (2011):1262–1266. http://doi.org/10.1073/pnas.1015316108

Dehaene, S. and J. P. Changeux. "Reward-Dependent Learning in Neuronal Networks for Planning and Decision-Making." *Cognition, Emotion and Autonomic Responses: The Integrative Role Of the Prefrontal Cortex and Limbic Structures*, eds. H. B. M. Uylings, C. G. van Eden, J. P. D. de Bruin, M. G. P. Feenstra, and C. M. A. Pennartz. New York: Elsevier, 2000. 219–230.

Diamond, Jared. *Guns, Germs, and Steel: The Fates of Human Societies*. New York: W.W. Norton, 1997.

Dolcos F., Y. Katsumi, M. Weymar, M. Moore, T. Tsukiura, and S. Dolcos. "Emerging Directions in Emotional Episodic Memory." *Frontiers in Psychology* 8 (December 4, 2017):1867. http://doi.org/10.3389/fpsyg.2017.01867

Drake, H. A. "The Impact of Constantine on Christianity." *The Cambridge Companion to the Age of Constantine*, ed. Noel Lenski. Cambridge: Cambridge University Press, 2005. 111–136. http://doi.org/10.1017/CCOL0521818389.006

Durkheim, Emile. *The Elementary Forms of the Religious Life*. New York: The Free Press, 1954. (Originally published in 1915).

Eller, Jack David. *Cruel Creeds, Virtuous Violence*. New York: Prometheus Books, 2010.

Evans-Pritchard, E. E. *The Nuer*. London: Pantianos Classics, 1940.

Ferguson, Christopher J., Allen Copenhaver, and Patrick Markey. "Reexamining the Findings of the American Psychological

Association's 2015 Task Force on Violent Media: A Meta-Analysis." Perspectives on Psychological Science 15/6 (2020):1423–1443. http://doi.org/10.1177/1745691620927666

Fischer, Ronald, Rohan Callander, Paul Reddish, and Joseph Bulbulia. "How Do Rituals Affect Cooperation? An Experimental Field Study Comparing Nine Ritual Types." *Human Nature* 24 (2013):115–125. http://doi.org/10.1007/s12110-013-9167-y

Flor-Henry, Pierre, Yakov Shapiro, and Corine Sombrun. "Brain Changes During a Shamanic Trance: Altered Modes of Consciousness, Hemispheric Laterality, and Systemic Psychobiology." *Cogent Psychology* 4:1 (2017). http://doi.org/10.1080/23311908.2017.1313522

Garrison, K. A., T. A. Zeffiro, D. Scheinost, et al. "Meditation Leads to Reduced Default Mode Network Activity Beyond an Active Task." *Cognitive and Affective Behavioral Neuroscience* 15 (2015):712–720. http://doi.org/10.3758/s13415-015-0358-3

Georgiev, A. V., A. C. E. Klimczuk, D. M. Traficonte, and D. Maestripieri. "When Violence Pays: A Cost-Benefit Analysis of Aggressive Behavior in Animals and Humans." *Evolutionary Psychology* 11/3 (2013):678–699. http://doi.org/10.1177/147470491301100313

Gibbons, Ann. "Thousands of Horsemen May Have Swept into Bronze Age Europe, Transforming the Local Population." *Science* (February 21, 2017). http://doi.org/10.1126/science aaI0806

Gini, Gianluca, Tiziana Pozzoli, and Shelley Hymel. "Moral Disengagement Among Children and Youth." *Aggressive Behavior* 40/1 (January 2014):56–68.

Girard, Rene. *Violence and the Sacred*. Trans. Patrick Gregory. Baltimore: Johns Hopkins University Press, 1977.

Glucklich, Ariel. *Sacred Pain*. New York: Oxford University Press, 2001.

Gomez, Jose Maria, Miguel Verdu, Adela Gozalex-Megias, and Marcos Mendez. "The Phylogenetic Roots of Human Lethal Violence." *Nature* 53 (2016):233–237. http://doi.org/10.1038/nature19758

Greenough, W. T. "What's Special About Development? Thoughts on the Bases of Experience Sensitive Synaptic Plasticity." In *Developmental Neuropsychobiology*, eds. W. T. Greenough and J. M. Juraska. New York: Academic Press, 1986. 387–408.

Greicius M. D., V. Kiviniemi, O. Tervonen, et al. "Persistent Default-Mode Network Connectivity During Light Sedation." *Human Brain Mapping* 29/7 (July 2008):839–847. http://doi.org/10.1002/hbm.20537

Greuel, Peter. "The Leopard Skin Chief: An Examination of Political Power Among the Nuer." *American Anthropologist* 73 (1971):1115–1120.

Gunz, Phillip, Simon Neubauer, Lubov Golovanova, et al. "A Uniquely Modern Human Pattern of Endocranial Development. Insights from a New Cranial Reconstruction of the Neandertal Newborn from Mezmaiskaya." *Journal of Human Evolution* 62/2 (2012):300–313. http://doi.org/10.1016/j.jhevol.2011.11.013

Guthrie, S. E. *Faces in the Clouds: A New Theory of Religion.* New York: Oxford University Press, 2003.

Haller, Jozsef and Menno R. Kruk. "Neuroendocrine Stress Responses and Aggression." In *Neurobiology of Aggression*, ed. Mark P. Mattson. New Jersey: Humana Press, 2003. 93–118.

Hammel, E. A. "Demographic Dynamics and Kinship in Anthropological Populations." *Proceedings of the National Academy of Sciences* 102 (2005):2248–2253. Print.

Hayden, Brian. "Alliances and Ritual Ecstasy: Human Responses to Resource Stress." *Journal for the Scientific Study of Religion* 26 1987:81–91.

Henshilwood, C. S., F. d'Errico, C. W. Marean, R. G. Milo, and R. Yates. "An Early Bone Tool Industry from the Middle Stone Age at Blombos

Cave, South Africa: Implications for the Origins of Modern Human Behaviour, Symbolism, and Language." *Journal of Human Evolution* 41 (2001):631–678.

Higley, J.D. and M. Linnoila. "Low Central Nervous System Serotonergic Activity is Traitlike and Correlates with Impulsive Behavior. A Nonhuman Primate Model Investigating Genetic and Environmental Influences on Neurotransmission." *Annals of the New York Academy of Sciences* 836/1 (1997):39–56. https://doi.org/10.1111/j.1749-6632 .1997.tb52354.x

Hirokawa, Eri and Hideki Ohira. "The Effects of Music Listening after a Stressful Task on Immune Functions, Neuroendocrine Responses, and Emotional States in College Students." *Journal of Music Therapy* 40/3 (Fall 2003):189–211. http://doi.org/10.1093/jmt/40.3.189

Hobson, Nicholas M., Juliana Schroeder, Jane L. Risen, Dimitris Xygalatas, and Michael Inzlicht. "The Psychology of Rituals: An Integrative Review and Process-Based Framework." *Personality and Social Psychology Review* 22/3 (2018):260–284. http://doi.org/10.1177/1088868317734944

Hove, M. J. and J. L. Risen. "It's All in the Timing: Interpersonal Synchrony Increases Affiliation. *Social Cognition* 27/6 (2007):949–961. http://doi.org/10.1521/soco.2009.27.6.949

Hudson, R. A. *The Sociology and Psychology of Terrorism: Who Becomes a Terrorist and Why?* A report prepared under an interagency agreement by the Federal Research Division, Library of Congress, September 1999. Retrieved December 2011, from www.loc.gov/rr/frd/pdf-files/Soc_ Psych_of_Terrorism.pdf

Hurlemann, René, A. Patin, O. Onur, et al. "Oxytocin Enhances Amygdala-Dependent, Socially Reinforced Learning and Emotional Empathy in Humans." *The Journal of Neuroscience : The Official Journal of the Society for Neuroscience* 30/14 (2010): 4999–5007. http://doi.org/ 10.1523/JNEUROSCI.5538-09.2010

Juergensmeyer, Mark. *Terror in the Mind of God: The Global Rise in Religious Violence*. Berkeley: University of California Press, 2003.

Juergensmeyer, Mark. *From Bhindranwale to bin Laden: The Rise of Religious Violence*. Tempe, AZ: Presentation at Arizona State University, (October 14–15, 2004a).

Juergensmeyer, Mark. "Holy Orders: Opposition to Modern States." *Harvard International Review* 25 (2004b):34–38.

Johnson, Dominic. *God is Watching You*. New York: Oxford University Press, 2016.

Johnson, M. "Functional Brain Development in Humans." *Nature Reviews Neuroscience* 2 (2001):475–483. http://doi.org/10.1038/35081509

Kaufman, J. and D. Charney. "Effects of Early Stress on Brain Structure and Function: Implications for Understanding the Relationship Between Child Maltreatment and Depression." *Development and Psychopathology* 13/3 (2001):451–471. http://doi.org/10.1017/S0954579401003030

Keeley, Lawrence H. *War Before Civilization: The Myth of the Peaceful Savage*. New York: Oxford University Press, 1996.

Kelemen D. "Are Children 'Intuitive Theists'? Reasoning About Purpose and Design in Nature." *Psychological Science* 15/5 (2004):295–301. http://doi.org/10.1111/j.0956-7976.2004.00672.x

Kellner, Michael, Christoph Muhtz, Asa Weinas, et al. "Impact of Physical or Sexual Childhood Abuse on Plasma DHEA, DHEA-S and Cortisol in a Low-Dose Dexamethasone Suppression Test and on Cardiovascular Risk Parameters in Adult Patients with Major Depression or Anxiety Disorders." *Psychiatry Research* 270 (2018):744–748.

Kiper, Jordan and Richard Sosis . "The Roots of Intergroup Conflict and the Co-option of the Religious System: An Evolutionary Perspective on Religious Terrorism." In *Oxford Handbook of Evolutionary Perspectives on Religion*, eds. J. Liddle and T. Shackelford. Oxford: Oxford University Press, 2021. 265–281.

Kirkpatrick, L. A. "Toward an Evolutionary Psychology of Religion and Personality." *Journal of Personality* 67 (1999):921–951.

Kitts, Margo. "The Last Night: Ritualized Violence and the Last Instructions of 9/11." *Journal of Religion* 90/3 (2010):283–312.

Koenig, H. G. *Medicine, Religion, and Health: Where Science and Spirituality Meet.* West Conshohocken, PA: Templeton Foundation Press, 2008.

Kosfeld, M., M. Heinrichs, P. J. Zak, U. Fischbacher, and E. Fehr. "Oxytocin Increases Trust in Humans." *Nature* 435/7042 (2005):673–676.

Krebs, J. R. and R. Dawkins. "Animal Signals: Mind-Reading and Manipulation." In *Behavioural Ecology: An Evolutionary Approach*, 2nd ed., eds. R. Krebs and N. B. Davies. Oxford: Blackwell Scientific Publications, 1984. 380–402.

Krumhansl, C. L. "An Exploratory Study of Musical Emotions and Psychophysiology." *Canadian Journal of Experimental Psychology* 51 (1997):336–353.

Lahr, M. M., F. Rivera, R. K. Power, et al. "Inter-group Violence Among Early Holocene Hunter-Gatherers of West Turkana, Kenya." *Nature* 529/7586 (2016):394–398.

Lansford, Jennifer E. "Development of Aggression." *Current Opinion in Psychology* 19 (2018):17–21.

Lebedev, Alexander V., Martin Lovden, Gidon Rosenthal, Amanda Feilding, David J. Nutt, and Robin L. Carhart-Harris. "Finding the Self by Losing the Self: Neural Correlates of Ego-Dissolution Under Psilocybin." *Human Brain Mapping* 36 (2015):3137–3153.

LeDoux, J. E. *The Emotional Brain.* New York: Simon and Schuster, 1996.

Lesch, Klaus Peter. "The Serotonergic Dimension of Aggression and Violence." In *Neurobiology of Aggression*, ed. Mark P. Mattson. New Jersey: Humana Press, 2003. 33–64.

Levenson R. W. "Blood, Sweat, and Fears: The Autonomic Architecture of Emotion." *Annals of the New York Academy of Sciences* 1000 (December 2003):348–366.

Levitin, David. *The World in Six Songs*. New York: Penguin Books, 2008.

Lincoln, B. *Holy Terrors: Thinking About Religion After September 11.* Chicago: University Of Chicago Press, 2003.

Luhrmann, Tanya. *When God Talks Back*. New York: Vintage Books, 2012.

Lutkehaus, N. C. and P. B. Roscoe. "Preface." In *Gender Rituals: Female Initiation in Melanesia*, eds. N. C. Lutkehaus and P. B. Roscoe. New York: Routledge, 1995. xiii–xix.

Lutz, Catherine and Geoffrey White. "The Anthropology of Emotions." *Annual Review of Anthropology* 15 (1986):405–436. http://doi.org/10.1146/annurev.an.15.100186.002201

Marean, C. W. "When the Sea Saved Humanity." *Scientific American* 303 (2010):54–61. Print.

Marques A. H., M. N. Silverman, and E. M. Sternberg. "Glucocorticoid Dysregulations and Their Clinical Correlates. From Receptors to Therapeutics." *Annals of the New York Academy of Sciences* 1179/1 (October 2009):1–18. http://doi.org/10.1111/j.1749-6632.2009.04987.x

McCullough M. E., W. T. Hoyt, D. B. Larson, H. G. Koenig, and C. Thoresen. "Religious Involvement and Mortality: A Meta-Analytic Review." *Health Psychology* 19/3 (May 2000):211–222.

Mohammadi, Bahram, Gregor R. Szycik, Bertte Wildt, et al. "Structural Brain Changes in Young Males Addicted to Video-Gaming." *Brain and Cognition* 139 (2020). http://doi.org/10.1016/j.bandc.2020.105518 (www.sciencedirect.com/science/article/pii/S027826261930199X)

Myerhoff, Barbara G. *Peyote Hunt: The Sacred Journey of the Huichol Indians*. Ithaca, NY: Cornell University Press, 1974.

Nesser, P. "How Did Europe's Global Jihadis Obtain Training for Their Militant Causes?" *Terrorism and Political Violence* 20 (2008):234–256.

Neubauer, Simon, Jean-Jacques Hublin, and Philipp Gunz. "The Evolution of Modern Human Brain Shape." *Science Advances* 4/1 (January 2018): eaao5961. http://doi.org/10.1126/sciadv.aao5961

Norenzayan, Ara. *Big Gods: How Religion Transformed Cooperation and Conflict*. New Jersey: Princeton University Press, 2013.

Otto, Rudolf. *The Idea of the Holy*. Translated by H. Milford. Oxford: Oxford University Press, 1923.

Oxford English Dictionary. "violence, n. 1a." OED Online. 2nd ed. Oxford: Oxford University Press, 1989. www.oed.com/oed2/00277885.

Paige, K. E. and J. M. Paige. *The Politics of Reproductive Ritual*. Los Angeles, CA: University of California Press, 1981.

Pape, R. *Dying to Win: The Strategic Logic of Suicide Terrorism*. New York: Random House, 2005.

Peltonen, K., N. Ellonen, J. Pitkänen, M. Aaltonen, and P. Martikainen. "Trauma and Violent Offending Among Adolescents: A Birth Cohort Study." *Journal of Epidemiology and Community Health* 74/10 (October 2020):845–850. http://doi.org/10.1136/jech-2020-214188

Pessiglione M., P. Petrovic, J. Daunizeau, et al. "Subliminal Instrumental Conditioning Demonstrated in the Human Brain." *Neuron* 59/4 (August 2008):561–567. http://doi.org/10.1016/j.neuron.2008.07.005

Pew Research Center. "When Americans Say They Believe in God, What Do They Mean?" Pew Research Center (Report April 25, 2018). www.pewresearch.org.

Pinker, Steven. *The Better Angels of Our Nature*. New York: Penguin Books, 2011.

Pollan, Michael. *How to Change Your Mind*. New York: Penguin Press, 2018.

Prüfer, K., K. Munch, I. Hellmann, et al. "The Bonobo Genome Compared with the Chimpanzee and Human Genomes." *Nature* 486 (2012):527–531. http://doi.org/10.1038/nature11128.PMID:22722832

Purzycki, B.G. and R. Sosis. *Religion Evolving: Cultural, Cognitive, and Ecological Dynamics*. Bristol, CT: Equinox, 2022.

Pusey, Anne E. and Kara Schroepfer-Walker. "Female Competition in Chimpanzees." *Philosophical Transactions of the Royal Society of London. Series B, Biological Sciences* 368/631 (October 2013): 1–12. http://doi.org/10.1098/rstb.2013.0077

Rappaport, R. A. "The Sacred in Human Evolution." *Annual Review of Ecology and Systematics* 2 (1971):23–44.

Rappaport, R. A. *Pigs for the Ancestors: Ritual in the Ecology of a New Guinea People*, 2nd ed. New Haven, CT: Yale University Press, 1984.

Rappaport, R. A. *Ritual and Religion in the Making of Humanity*. London: Cambridge University Press, 1999.

Rimmele, Ulrike, K. Hediger, M. Heinrichs, and P. Klaver. "Oxytocin Makes a Face in Memory Familiar." *The Journal of Neuroscience: The Official Journal of the Society for Neuroscience* 29/1 (2009):38–42. http://doi.org/10.1523/JNEUROSCI.4260-08.2009

Ross H. E. and L. J. Young. "Oxytocin and the Neural Mechanisms Regulating Social Cognition and Affiliative Behavior." *Frontiers in Neuroendocrinology* 30/4 (2009):534–547. http://doi.org/10.1016/j.yfrne.2009.05.004

Rowe, C. "Receiver Psychology and the Evolution of Multi-Component Signals." *Animal Behaviour* 58/5 (1999):921–931.

St Onge, J. and S. Floresco. "Dopaminergic Modulation of Risk-Based Decision Making." *Neuropsychopharmacology* 34 (2009):681–697. https://doi.org/10.1038/npp.2008.121

Sala, N., A. Pantoja-Perez, A. Gracia, and J. L. Arsuaga. "Taphonomic-Forensic Analysis of the Hominin Skulls From the Sima de los Huesos." *The Anatomic Record of the American Association for Anatomy*, Special Issue Article, February (2022). http://doi.org/10.1002/ar.24883

Sapolsky, R. M. "Why Stress is Bad for Your Brain." *Science* 273 (1996):749–750.

Saver, J. L. and J. Rabin. "The Neural Substrates of Religious Experience." *Journal of Neuropsychiatry* 9 (1997):498–520.

Scherer, K. R. and M. R. Zentner. "Emotional Effects of Music: Production Rules." In *Music and Emotion*, eds. P. Juslin and J. Sloboda. Oxford: Oxford University Press, 2001. 361–392.

Schlegel, A. and H. Barry, III. "The Evolutionary Significance of Adolescent Initiation Ceremonies." *American Ethnologist* 7/4 (1980):696–715. http://doi.org/10.1525/ae.1980.7.4.02a00060

Shariff, A. F. and M. Rhemtulla. "Divergent Effects of Beliefs in Heaven and Hell on National Crime Rates." *PLoS ONE* 7/6 (2012):e39048. http://doi.org/10.1371/journal.pone.0039048

Sharp, P. B., B. P. Sutton, E. J. Paul, et al. "Mindfulness Training Induces Structural Connectome Changes in Insula Networks." *Science Reports* 8/1 (2018): 7929. http://doi.org/10.1038/s41598-018-26268-w

Sosis, Richard. "Religious Behaviors, Badges, and Bans: Signaling Theory and the Evolution of Religion." In *Where God and Science Meet: How Brain and Evolutionary Studies Alter Our Understanding of Religion (Vol. 1): Evolution, Genes, and the Religious Brain*, ed. Patrick McNamara. Westport, CT: Praeger Publishers/Greenwood Publishing Group, 2006. 77–102.

Sosis, Richard. "The Building Blocks of Religious Systems: Approaching Religion as a Complex Adaptive System." In *Evolution, Development & Complexity: Multiscale Models of Complex Adaptive System*s, eds. Georgi Yordanov Georgiev, John M. Smart, Claudio L. Flores Martinez, and Michael Price. New York: Springer, 2019. 421–449.

Sosis, Richard. "Four Advantages of a Systemic Approach to the Study of Religion." *Archive for the Psychology of Religion* 42/1 (2020):142–157.

Sosis, Richard and Candace Alcorta. "Signaling, Solidarity, and the Sacred: The Evolution of Religious Behavior." *Evolutionary Anthropology* 12 (2003):264–274.

Sosis, Richard and Candace S. Alcorta. "Militants and Martyrs: Evolutionary Perspectives on Religion and Terrorism." In *Natural Security: A Darwinian Approach to a Dangerous World*, eds. R. Sagarin and T. Taylor. Los Angeles, CA: University of California Press, 2008. 105–124.

Sosis, Richard and Eric Bressler. "Cooperation and Commune Longevity: A Test of the Costly Signaling Theory of Religion." *Cross-Cultural Research* 37 (2003):211–239.

Sosis, Richard and Joseph Bulbulia. "The Behavioral Ecology of Religion: The Benefits and Costs of One Evolutionary Approach," *Religion* 41/3 (2011):341–362. http://doi.org/10.1080/0048721X.2011.604514

Sosis, Richard and W. Penn Handwerker. "Psalms and Coping with Uncertainty: Religious Israeli Women's Responses to the 2006 Lebanon War." *American Anthropologist* 113/1 (2011):40–55.

Sosis, Richard and Bradley Ruffle. "Religious Ritual and Cooperation: Testing for a Relationship on Israeli Religious and Secular Kibbutzim." *Current Anthropology* 44 (2003):713–722.

Sosis, Richard and Bradley Ruffle. "Religion, and the Evolution of Cooperation: Field Experiments on Israeli Kibbutzim." *Research in Economic Anthropology* 23 (2004):87–115.

Sosis, Richard, Howard Kress, and James Boster. "Scars for War: Evaluating Alternative Signaling Explanations for Cross-Cultural Variance in Ritual Costs." *Evolution and Human Behavior* 28 (2007):234–247.

Sosis, Richard, Erika J. Phillips, and Candace S. Alcorta. "Sacrifice and Sacred Values: Evolutionary Perspectives on Religious Terrorism." In *The Oxford Handbook of Evolutionary Perspectives on Violence, Homicide, and War*, eds. Todd K. Shackelford and Viviana A. Weekes-Shackelford. New York: Oxford University Press, 2012. 233–253. http://doi.org/10.1093/oxfordhb/9780199738403.013.0014

Spear, Linda P. "The Adolescent Brain and Age-Related Behavioral Manifestations." *Neuroscience and Biobehavioral Reviews* 24 (2000):417–463.

Strathern, Andrew and Pamela J. Stewart. "Introduction: Terror, The Imagination, and Cosmology." In *Terror and Violence: Imagination and the Unimaginable*, eds. Andrew Strathern, Pamela J. Stewart and Neil L. Whitehead. London: Pluto Press, 2005. 1–39.

Sutton, Donald S. "Rituals of Self-Mortification: Taiwanese Spirit-Mediums in Comparative Perspective." *Journal of Ritual Studies* 4/1 (1990): 99–125.

Swanson, G. *The Birth of the Gods*. Ann Arbor, MI: University of Michigan Press, 1960

Tafet, G. E., V. P. Idoyaga-Vargas, D. P. Abulafia, et al. "Correlation Between Cortisol Level and Serotonin Uptake in Patients with Chronic Stress and Depression. *Cognitive, Affective, and Behavioral Neuroscience* 1/4 (2001):388–393. http://doi.org/10.3758/cabn.1.4.388. PMID:12467090.

Teicher, M. H., S. L. Andersen, A. Polcari, et al. "The Neurobiological Consequences of Early Stress and Childhood Maltreatment." *Neuroscience Biobehavioral Reviews* 27/1–2 (2003):33–44. http://doi.org/10.1016/s0149-7634(03)00007-1. PMID: 12732221.

Teicher, M., J. Samson, C. Anderson, et al. "The Effects of Childhood Maltreatment on Brain Structure, Function and Connectivity." *Nature Reviews Neuroscience* 17 (2016):652–666. http://doi.org/10.1038/nrn.2016.111

Thorpe, I. J. N. "Anthropology, Archaeology, and the Origin of Warfare." *World Archaeology*, 35/1 (2003):145–165.

Tinbergen, N. *The Study of Instinct*. Clarendon Press: Oxford, 1965.

Tooley, U. A., D. S. Bassett, and A. P. Mackey. "Environmental Influences on the Pace of Brain Development." *Nature Reviews Neuroscience* 22 (2021):372–384. http://doi.org/10.1038/s41583-021-00457-5

Turner, Victor. *The Ritual Process: Structure and Anti-Structure*. Chicago: Aldine, 1969.

Tuzin, Donald. *The Ilahita Arapesh: Dimensions of Unity*. Berkeley, CA: University of California Press, 1976.

Tylor, E. B. *Primitive Culture*. London: Murray, 1871.

Uvnas-Moberg, K. "Oxytocin May Mediate the Benefits of Positive Social Interaction and Emotions." *Psychoneuroendocrinology* 23/8 (1998):819–835.

Vaish, A., T. Grossmann, and A. Woodward. "Not All Emotions Are Created Equal: The Negativity Bias in Social-Emotional Development." *Psychological Bulletin* 134 (2008):383–403.

Valeri, Valerio. *Kingship and Sacrifice: Ritual and Society in Ancient Hawaii*. Translated by Paula Wissig. Chicago: University of Chicago Press, 1985.

van Gaal, Simon and Victor A. F. Lamme. "Unconscious High-Level Information Processing: Implication for Neurobiological Theories of Consciousness." *Neuroscientist* 18/3 (June 2012):287–301. http://doi.org/10.1177/1073858411404079.

Victoroff, J. "The Mind of the Terrorist: A Review and Critique of Psychological Approaches." *Journal of Conflict Resolution* 49 (2005):3–42.

Villani, Susan and Nandita Joshi. "Television and Movies, Rock Music and Music Videos, and Computer and Video Games: Understanding and Preventing Learned Violence in the Information Age." In *Neurobiology of Aggression*, ed. Mark P. Mattson. New Jersey: Humana Press, 2003. 231–252.

Wahlstrom, Dustin, Paul Collins, Tonya White, et al. "Developmental Changes in Dopamine Neurotransmission in Adolescence: Behavioral Implications and Issues in Assessment." *Brain and Cognition* 72/1 (2010): 146–59. http://doi.org/10.1016/j.bandc.2009.10.013

Wallace, Anthony F. C. *Religion: An Anthropological View*. New York: Random House, 1966.

Watts J., O. Sheehan, Q. D. Atkinson, J. Bulbulia, and R. D. Gray. "Ritual Human Sacrifice Promoted and Sustained the Evolution of Stratified Societies." *Nature* 532 (April 2016):228–231. http://doi.org/10.1038/nature17159

Whitehouse, Harvey. *Modes of Religiosity: A Cognitive Theory of Religious Transmission*. Walnut Creek, CA: Altamira Press, 2004.

Wilson, Michael Lawrence. "Environmental Factors and Aggression in Nonhuman Primates." In *Neurobiology of Aggression: Understanding and Preventing Violence*, ed. Mark P. Mattson. New Jersey: Humana Press, 2003. 167–190.

Wiltermuth S. S. and C. Heath. "Synchrony and Cooperation." *Psychological Science* 20/1 (2009):1–5. http://doi.org/10.1111/j.1467-9280.2008

Winkelman, Michael. "Trance States: A Theoretical Model and Cross-Cultural Analysis." *Ethos* 14 (1986):174–203.

Winkelman, Michael. *Shamanism: The Neural Ecology of Consciousness and Healing*. Westport, CT: Bergin and Garvey, 2000.

World Health Organization. *World Report on Violence and Health*. Geneva: World Health Organization, 2002.

Wrangham, Richard W. "Two Types of Aggression in Human Evolution." *Proceedings of the National Academies of Science* 115/2 (2018):245–253.

Wrangham, Richard W. *The Goodness Paradox*. New York: Pantheon Books, 2019.

Wrangham R. W. and L. Glowacki. "Intergroup Aggression in Chimpanzees and War in Nomadic Hunter-Gatherers: Evaluating the Chimpanzee Model." *Human Nature* 23/1 (2012):5–29. http://doi.org/10.1007/s12110-012-9132-1.PMID:22388773.

Wright, Robin M. "Assault Sorcery." *Oxford Handbooks Online*. Oxford: Oxford University Press, 2015. http://doi.org/10.1093/oxfordhb/9780199935420.013.28

Xygalatas, Dimitris, Panagiotis Mitkidis, Ronald Fischer, et al. "Extreme Rituals Promote Prosociality." *Psychological Science* 24/8 (2013):1602–1605. http://doi.org/10.1177/0956797612472910

Zahavi, A. "Mate Selection: A Selection for a Handicap." *Journal of Theoretical Biology* 53 (1975):205–214.

Zhou, Feng, Christian Montag, Rayna Sariyska, et al. "Orbitofrontal Gray Matter Deficits as Marker of Internet Gaming Disorder: Converging Evidence from a Cross-Sectional and Prospective Longitudinal Design." *Addiction Biology* 24/1 (2019):100–109. http://doi.org/10.1111/adb.12570

Zhu, Wenfeng, Xiaolin Zhou, and Ling-Sizng Xia. "Brain Structures and Functional Connectivity Associated with Individual Differences in Trait Proactive Aggression." *Nature Scientific Reports* 9 (2019):7731. http://doi.org/10.1038/s41598-019-44115-4

Zollikofer, Christoph P. E., Marcia S. Ponce de Leon, Bernard Vandermeersch, and Francois Leveque. "Evidence for Interpersonal Violence in the St. Cesaire Neanderthal." *Proceedings of the National Academy of Sciences* 99/9 (April 2002):6444–6448. http://doi.org/10.1073/pnas.082111899

Cambridge Elements ☰

Religion and Violence

James R. Lewis
Wuhan University

James R. Lewis is Professor at Wuhan University, and the
author and editor of a number of volumes, including *The
Cambridge Companion to Religion and Terrorism*.

Margo Kitts
Hawai'i Pacific University

Margo Kitts edits the *Journal of Religion and Violence* and is
Professor and Coordinator of Religious Studies and East-West
Classical Studies at Hawai'i Pacific University in Honolulu.

ABOUT THE SERIES

Violence motivated by religious beliefs has become all too common
in the years since the 9/11 attacks. Not surprisingly, interest in the
topic of religion and violence has grown substantially since then.
This Elements series on Religion and Violence addresses this new,
frontier topic in a series of ca. fifty individual Elements.
Collectively, the volumes will examine a range of topics, including
violence in major world religious traditions, theories of religion
and violence, holy war, witch hunting, and human sacrifice,
among others.

Cambridge Elements ≡

Religion and Violence

Printed in the United States
by Baker & Taylor Publisher Services